CRICKET
WITHOUT A CAUSE

For David

nuff respect

Hilary 28/9/17.

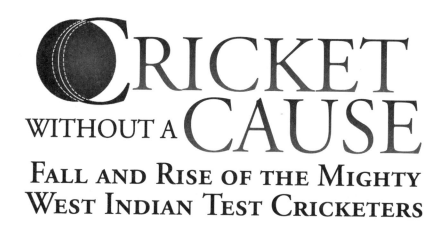

CRICKET

WITHOUT A CAUSE

FALL AND RISE OF THE MIGHTY WEST INDIAN TEST CRICKETERS

Hilary McD. Beckles

IAN RANDLE PUBLISHERS
Kingston • Miami

First published in Jamaica, 2017 by
Ian Randle Publishers
16 Herb McKenley Drive
Box 686
Kingston 6, Jamaica W.I.
www.ianrandlepublishers.com

© 2017 Hilary McD. Beckles

ISBN: 978-976-637-952-0 (hbk)
       978-976-637-960-5 (pbk)

National Library of Jamaica Cataloguing-In-Publication Data

Beckles, Hilary McD.
    Cricket without a cause: fall and rise of the mighty West Indian test
    cricketers / Hilary McD. Beckles

        pages; cm
Includes bibliographical references
ISBN 978-976-637-952-0

1 Cricket player – West Indies.
2. Cricket – West Indies – History.
3. Cricket – Social aspects – West Indies.
4. Cricket – Statistics.
5. Cricket players.
I. Title

796.358092 - dc 23

Cover and book design by Ian Randle Publishers
Printed and bound in the United Kingdom

Dedication

For Elisha St. Charles MacAndrew Beckles,
my four-year-old grandson, a passionate player,
and his generation of West Indian (Windies) cricketers.

Contents

SECTION 3: RETURN OF THE WEST INDIES

List of Tables

Acronyms and Abbreviations

BBC	British Broadcasting Corporation
BCA	Barbados Cricket Association
BCCI	Board of Control for Cricket in India
CARICOM	Caribbean Community
CCC	Combined Campuses and Colleges
CRC	Cricket Research Centre
CWI	Cricket West Indies
HPC	High Performance Centre
ICC	International Cricket Council
IMF	International Monetary Fund
IPL	Indian Premier League
MCC	Marylebone Cricket Club
NGO	Non-governmental Organization
ODI	One Day International
UWI	The University of the West Indies
WICB	West Indies Cricket Board
WICBC	West Indies Cricket Board of Control
WIPA	West Indies Players' Association

Prologue

The fall of West Indian Test cricket performance from global dominance at the end of the twentieth century was as dramatic and spectacular as its rise 50 years earlier. In less than five years, beginning in 1995, with the Test series defeat by Australia, the maroon clad cricketers (Windies) descended from an awesome altitude into the awful abyss in which it now finds itself. The calamity befell both cricketers and administrators. Within the boundary and in the boardroom, Windies reputation was ripped and ruined. The loss of prestige was painful and is now persistent. In global competitive terms, the experience was registered as a cultural shock, a catastrophic setback for the Caribbean nation.

The sudden, unpredicted loss of competitive excellence is considered one of modernity's most cataclysmic cultural occurrences. The rise in the late 1970s was associated with stunning, breathtaking, personal performances and incredible team achievements. Equally, the fall has been described in terms of a shocking display of individual ineptitude and indiscipline, and collective indifference and irresponsibility. The West Indies Cricket Board (WICB), now Cricket West Indies (CWI) once seen as flexible and creative in producing excellent results, is now considered a blunt, blustering instrument of corporate power without community purpose.

The rise and rule of the Windies was undoubtedly the most perfectly executed collective project of the politically fragmented Caribbean nation. It entered, endured and eventually dominated international cricket in all its forms. The world marvelled at the extraordinary success because it was conceptualized and implemented by a colonized community of a few million people and sustained by a young, ambitious, though politically divisive community.

The statistical odds and historical forces were stacked against the success of the officials and cricketers. For many observers at home and abroad, it seemed an impossible mission. But it was carefully crafted in the progressive consciousness of brilliant cricketers, perfected by their passion for justice and freedom, and sustained by the societal impulses for radical self-liberation.

Coming to the crease in the oppressiveness of nineteenth-century colonialism, and bred in the anti-colonialism of the early twentieth century, Windies cricket was born with a soul dedicated to democratic transformation. These political values and ideological sensibility constituted its heart and soul. Through these eyes the world witnessed the desire of a people for justice, equality and dignity. Communities everywhere, free and colonized, identified with Windies as a social movement for good and were stimulated by its imagination. They became a part of its journey.

The soul of the Windies, then, was forged and matured within a specific ideological context and was put to work on behalf of the eruptive, egalitarian demand of the twentieth-century world. It was this soul that enabled its finest cricketers and administrators to stand in the face of personal and collective injustice and mobilize their Caribbean identity in the service of a progressive humanity.

From George Headley to Learie Constantine before the Second World War, to Frank Worrell, Everton Weekes, Clyde Walcott, Sonny Ramadin and Alfred Valentine after it, and on to Wes Hall, Rohan Kanhai, Gary Sobers, Clive Lloyd, Viv Richards, Malcolm Marshall, Courtney Walsh and Michael Holding, the soul of West Indies cricket was represented by heroic players who understood and advocated for freedom, equality and justice within the context of the global democracy movement.

The Windies soul, then, provided an energy source that empowered an unrelenting determination to achieve fairness and justice. Critically, it demanded that each person had a right to opportunity, and to perform within the humanist framework that celebrated excellence. Within this philosophical context it drew upon an inexhaustible source of performance energy, pride and social dignity. Players and administrators, as host of the soul, mastered, transformed and dominated the Test game during the last quarter of the twentieth century. No other nation has ever been so dominant. Windies redefined performance standards and reshaped the sport before adoring spectators. They became the standard bearers of the post-colonial game.

The forces of political opposition soon descended and sought to eliminate the illumination. Along with the persistent support of national and global spectators came the inevitable envy of backroom executives who occupied positions of power beyond the boundary. In some boardrooms there was rage – born of jealousy and poor sportsmanship. An anti-Windies mentality took time to make its presence felt, but eventually it spawned a campaign to undermine Windies' influence and reverse its record of attainment.

After two decades of dominance (1976–96) successive defeats tore the outer core of the Caribbean soul. By 1998, Windies were free falling into systemic decline. Despair took root along the route, and like most things of great value it was placed like a commodity on sale. Marginalized within the game's money market and its legacy devalued in the boardroom of the International Cricket Council (ICC), Windies wilted. Under pressures of persistent performance penalties, racial antagonism and sustained financial subversion, the 'men in maroon' and those in the boardroom minimised their political and ideological inheritance and went to market with a 'cash before country' engagement outlook.

But no global sale is ever without a local collaborator. A few well-placed and commercially connected Caribbean cricketers and administrators facilitated the conveyances and were willing business participants. The 'rebel tours' of the mid-1980s to apartheid South

Africa brought them to the fore though they had preferred to remain in the shadow. By the end of the 1990s, their mercantile transactions were more visible and treacherous. The Windies soul was torn from the nationalist scaffold and sold. Thereafter, the fall from grace to a lowly Test place is a tale best told as the sale of the Windies soul.

The process began dialectically when the WICB reinvented itself as a fully corporate force. The soul of Windies was now seen as a global asset whose national retention was financially unsound. The rise of Pat Rousseau's regime in 1996 saw the final maturity of this transition. Given a mandate to commercialize Windies cricket, and to lead a corporate revolution to generate wealth for its stakeholders, President Rousseau, one of many former presidents drawn from the business community, effectively though inadvertently unleashed the understanding within Windies that it required 'cash to care' for Test cricket. The WICB set the new standard for cashing in, and in a series of sponsorship deals bartered the soul of the Windies to culturally insensitive commercial bidders. The players took note and feeling marginalized in Rousseau new money generating paradigm, prepared to strike out. 'Cash before country', the players said, was the WICB creation. They took up the concept and ran with it.

The first signs of Windies 'nation-cricket' being placed on the backburners had appeared on South Africa's apartheid auction blocks. Between 1982 and 1984, teams of fine Windies cricketers, mostly African and few Asian descended, contracted to play and lived in the white supremacy land as 'honorary whites'. Dubbed the 'rebel tours' by the international community, the games they played and the life they lived provided an opportunity for the return to a dark commercial past in which the black body became the property of whites investors. The global democracy movement and the soul of Windies cricket began to haemorrhage.

The second phase of the sale of the soul took place during the 1998 Windies official Test tour to the now politically liberated South Africa. This was the Rousseau tour that finally pierced the body-politic and tore the soul from the torso. The WICB, now visibly a 'for profit organization', was reinvented and stripped of social awareness and political responsibility. Players, now embracing the new cash culture placed the tour on hold, went on strike for a few dollars more, snubbed President Mandela's welcome, ignored the clarion call of ghettoized black youth, and demanded assurances from Rousseau that 'cash before cricket' was the new deal. The team jettisoned its legacy of linkage to liberation and laid bare its bones before the new, commercial cricket. Now bereft of the soul that had propelled Test performance, Windies cricket took a turn for the worse, and was soon pronounced in a poorly state.

Stakeholders at home within the state and civil society seemed powerless to resist the sale. Dollarized and undervalued by the WICB, and dominated by 'cash first cricketers', Windies cricket was rendered fully vulnerable to be exploited by global capital and further marginalized within the International Cricket Council (ICC). Separated from its social energy, and buckled at the belly, Windies Test cricket fell to its knees. Having cast aside that which had made it unique and powerful, it descended to a place detached from national pride. In this void it was vanquished. Prostrated in posture it fell prey to the corporate dons of the global commercial game, and their insiders in the ICC.

The Windies fan was blinded by the bling of the glittering 'cash and carry' cricket culture. The greater good Windies Test performance once represented was bartered for the new glamour. Players rejected the heritage of the Test hero and desired instead the status of the star, a shining light that illuminated itself while casting dark shadows throughout the region.

Restoring the soul of Windies cricket is a necessary precondition for rebuilding its diminished Test brand. Without its soul reclaimed there can be no sustained excellence. In its absence, individual enrichment and collective poverty will persistently parade and prevail. As citizens prepare to negotiate the second phase of their nation-building project, they must rise up and take back their Test cricket. The struggle for the return and restoration of the Windies soul must be waged on all fronts – in educational institutions, political parties and governments, civil society, corporate boardrooms, media houses, and in stadia where fans must take a stand. Without this victory, there can be no return to Test glory.

Acknowledgements

I give thanks to C.L.R. James for his encouragement of my early effort. I am grateful for the many conversations with Michael Manley who believed at his end that there was a baton to be passed. Respect is offered to past and present Prime Ministers, P.J. Patterson, Owen Arthur, Ralph Gonsalves, Keith Mitchell and Keith Rowley who, on behalf of the Caribbean, are demanding explanations and accountability. Ken Gordon and Julian Hunte, as Presidents of WICB, invited my service. I was honoured for the opportunity to serve as an 'independent' director for four years. Vaneisa Baksh, Frank Birbalsingh, Simon Wilde, Brian Stoddart, Rob Steen, Keith Sandiford, Mike Marqusee, and Scyld Berry have written perceptively and persuasively on this subject. I offer respect and give thanks for their insights and interactions.

I have benefited from a carnival of cricket conversations with many Windies legends – Sir Everton Weekes, Sir Viv Richards, Sir Gary Sobers, Floyd Reifer, Clive Lloyd, Sir Andy Roberts, Joel Garner, Lance Gibbs, Jimmy Adams, Sir Wes Hall, Sir Curtly Ambrose, Darren Sammy, Courtney Walsh, Michael Holding, Ian Bishop, Desmond Haynes, Gordon Greenidge, Sir Richie Richardson, Michael Findlay, Brian Lara, Jeff Dujon, Shiv Chanderpaul, Maurice Foster, Hilary (Larry) Gomes, Malcolm Marshall, Carl Hooper, Rawle Brancker, Rohan Kanhai, Joey Carew and emerging icons Carlos Brathwaite and Jason Holder. I owe them more than I can ever say or repay. Camileta Neblett, Grace Jutan and Marvette Facey-Thompson, my executive assistants, worked diligently on the manuscript. I appreciate their support and kindness.

Introduction

CASH BEFORE COUNTRY: BOARDROOM TO LOCKER ROOM

Imagine this if you can! The year is 2030 and Jamaica is unable to gain an Olympic medal in the fast lane. Consider this, furthermore, that the iconic island's golden reputation for speed once represented by Usain Bolt, Elaine Thompson and Shelly-Ann Fraser Pryce – the fastest humans of all time – is routinely ridiculed and set aside as a relic of a deniable past. Agreed, no one can.

This was precisely the possibility pondered by pundits at the end of the twentieth century who tried to imagine Windies future status in Test. Like Jamaicans in global track today, Windies in the early 1990s assumed an aura of invincibility. Their dominance defied earthly gravitational laws. Successful teams rose to a place far above and beyond competitors, and at the crease were light years ahead. Indeed, so distant and dominant were these teams that they were described by experts as irretrievably launched into their own galaxy. But, not even the brightest star is ever static. Windies crashing descent to earth at the turn of the twenty-first century, not predicted by the pundits, must now be accounted for and explained.

The tale of the rise and rule of Windies has been brilliantly told by its finest scribes. From the incomparable C.L.R. James in the 1960s to monumental Michael Manley in the 1990s, the hectic flow of manuscripts energized the 'telling' industry. Windies excellence in Test was historicized as a journey of generations over a hundred years. They began as outsiders, less than underdogs, in their exploratory overseas tour to Canada and the USA in 1886. This was followed by 30 years of touring the UK as unofficial outfits and second class crusaders.

In 1927, after this long, gruelling, and sometimes humiliating apprenticeship, they were awarded Test status. The West Indies Cricket Board of Control (WICBC) was created in 1927 with a mandate to make internationally competitive the Windies team. By 1986, they were officially ranked the undisputed Test cricket champions. The WICBC had good reasons to be proud. Players and administrators had proven a powerful political point. With good management, a clear mandate and mission, a team could climb the tallest tree. The literature creatively captured the political consciousness and expectation of the Caribbean expedition. Critically, it surmised, the expertise of Windies in world Test could never be surpassed. Simply told, they were too large and in charge to fall.

The narrative was presented as an enterprise launched by the WICBC in three distinct phases. Each era is considered a rising. The first rising took place in 1948–51 when Windies, after defeating India (1948) and England (1950) in their own backyards, journeyed to Australia (1951) to capture the world title as best in Test. The quest failed but did not derail the determination. The second rising was seminal. Between 1963 and 1967, Windies defeated England twice, Australia for the first time, and India and claimed the Test title. It was a short-lived presence at the pinnacle. Defeated by England in 1968, they returned to the cauldron from whence they came. The third rising was revolutionary. Between 1978 and 1995, Windies attained and sustained global dominance.

My contribution to the narrative sought to map the magnificence of Windies mastery and to dramatize and detail the imagery of invincibility. In three edited texts, *An Area of Conquest* (1994), *Liberation Cricket* (1995) and *A Spirit of Dominance* (1998), I set out to consolidate the Jamesian paradigm that situated Test cricket performance, and its political ideology, within Caribbean anti-colonialism and the project of nation-building.

Before 1995, however, [when Windies were defeated by Australia at Sabina Park, Jamaica], I had seen a crack in the concrete. I ran into the street and warned the community. The WICBC was invited in 2000 to a two day seminar hosted by the University of the West Indies (UWI) in order to assess the evidence. Representatives came but no consensus was reached on the significance of the data. Gregory Shillingford, the CEO, understood very well what was at stake, but the Rousseau presidency was driven in an imbalanced way by the revenue-generating agenda while performances on the field were plummeting and creating a crisis in player attitudes.

The light that pierced through the crack enabled close observers to conceptualize the widening of the crevice, and in short time, the crumble. It took a while to ponder the evidence of things not generally seen nor discussed to realize the significance of the minor structural breach. My years of research that followed appeared in a two-volume 1998 monograph – *The Development of West Indies Cricket: Volume 1: The Age of Nationalism*, and *Volume 2: The Age of Globalization*.

My intention focused on the new, corrosive global transformations that were weakening Caribbean consciousness and political resolve, and subsequently subverting the Test cricket agenda. Initially, I remained optimistic that the crack could be corrected, the leak sealed and structural integrity restored. This was not to be. The crack became a catastrophe that created Caribbean dispair. Since then, I have examined the ruins from all angles. I remain enthusiastic that the edifice can and will be restored.

The process of reflection led to deeper engagement and activism. The University of the West Indies at its Cave Hill campus in Barbados had an important role to play through the CLR James Cricket Research Centre (CRC). Established in 1994, its mandate was clear and precise: to facilitate the sustainability of cricket excellence in the Caribbean and beyond. This meant, among other things, participating in the planning of the next era and the fourth rising of Windies in Test. As director of the Centre, I took this responsibility personally and professionally.

To this end, a Master's Degree in Cricket Studies was launched by the Centre; the first programme of its kind anywhere. This created comparative pedagogical perspective on the loss of Test excellence. The conviction to comprehend the causes of the crumbling was a central agenda item. Caribbean academia desperately wanted to get to the root of the reasons.

During the first two decades of Test performance decline, 1995–2015, I worked intimately with the rebranded WICB, (President Rousseau had removed the 'C' for control) to rethink its policies and strategies, and to focus on another crucial aspect of the systemic decline – the inadequate mental preparation of young cricketers and the strategic focus of administrators. The WICB agreed to invite a team of students from the tertiary education sector to participate in regional competitions. The team played as The Combined Campuses and Colleges (CCC), which so far has defeated all regional teams.

The UWI and WICB also agreed to work toward the establishment of a cricket academy upon the framework of the successful CCC. This facility emerged as the Sagicor–WICB High Performance Centre (HPC), and was also headquartered at the Cave Hill campus. As the inaugural Chairman of the HPC and non-territorial member of WICB, I was well placed to promote the integration of classroom discourses with on-field technical training for the next generation of cricketers. Today, two students of the CCC and the HPC, Jason Holder and Carlos Brathwaite, are captains of Windies Test and T20 teams respectively. They are the symbols of the success imagined, and the foundations on which Windies can rise for the fourth time.

This text, then, is a rejoinder to the conversation that began in the late 1990s about what went terribly wrong with Windies Test and how best to get it right. A few voices within the discourse have been enlightening but many have been rapacious. Meanwhile, the ruins remain a cruel reminder of what once was. Test defeats have become the norm and are no longer breaking news. The WICB, rebranded in 2017 as Cricket West Indies (CWI), is at odds with public opinion and political leaders. The more dramatic the grubbing, the greater the public impulse to impale those they considered responsible: the WICB and the last cohort of senior players.

To write is to risk a fall into the blame game that serves no other purpose than to widen and deepen the divide. Yet, it remains true that without accountability and responsibility there can be no preparation for the fourth rising. I offer this contribution to the conversation because it speaks as much to cricket concerns as it does to the development challenges facing the twenty-first-century Caribbean.

As West Indians, we are a small, financially challenged, politically fragmented, but fiercely focused cultural community that achieved with cricket in the last quarter of the twentieth century that which many large and richly endowed nations have failed to attain – world-class excellence and performance dominance. Emerging from a cruel colonial past we built with this game a respected structure to social survival and the attainment of political sovereignty. The loss of excellence is always an indication of diffused effort and a reflection of unfocused intention.

As the world prepares to lengthen its stride into this twenty-first century the reasons for the crumbled creation of an earlier generation should be confronted. Imploded in parts, but torn down in sections, it is a ruin of a once proud patrimony. While the decline was for a long time deniable, and the decay now vividly discernible, it is time to return to the site with a restorative intent and roadmap.

Increasingly poor Test performances suggest the truth; that Windies administrators and cricketers are no longer motivated to excitement by the format that is Test. Cricket administrators during the decline long responded to players with the application of obsolete rules and regulations rather than education and generated greater industrial relations insults than field results. Disillusioned in their dealings with the WICB, players rushed deeper into the pursuit of global gain while generating considerable local pain. The process was not without its technical consequences. Skill sets and

Cricket Without A Cause

fitness corroded while the relations between players and officials were typified by mutual suspicion and disrespect. Within the new culture of 'cash before country' is to be found the root cause of the fall from Test excellence.

In 2000, the CRC invited former British Prime Minister, John Major, to deliver the Sixth Annual Sir Frank Worrell Memorial Lecture at the Cave Hill Campus of the UWI. It was a delightful event in the company of the global cricket fraternity. The former prime minister spoke eloquently in celebration of Windies legacy, and expressed gratitude to its legends for the role they played in shaping his cultural awareness. Growing up in south London in the periphery of Kennington Oval – the heartland of the West Indian diaspora – he said, prepared him for the Windies journey. He admitted to being an irretrievable admirer of the soul of Windies cricket.

Conversations focused on the falter and fall of Windies Test quality. I reminded the prime minister that English Test cricket, after two decades of decline that began in the early 1970s, had produced similar effects upon the national consciousness. The English Test team was humiliated, and natives, fed up with the bloodletting, opted to stay at home. The British Broadcasting Corporation quietly reported the carnage. Weak Test teams and growing tele-crowds, I said to him, had become the English norm, and I feared the worst for the English game.

The prime minister was attentive. Then he dropped the bomb! 'Cricket culture, Professor,' he said, 'runs deep in British civilization. The root will search until water is found, and then we shall witness a flourish. I hope the same is true of the West Indies.'

Since then I have pondered his question. How deep are cricket roots in the West Indies? How long can the culture withstand this persistent drought? Major was profound and prophetic. English cricket has since soared. The rains fell and stars appeared.

Windies are approaching the end of their third decade of Test decline. Their competitors vow never again to allow them to regain their lost status. Memories of the golden age of glory are fast fading. Legends are drifting into the twilight. It is feared in some places that soon the evidence of the edifice will be erased from public consciousness and consigned to folk history. The past will become the preserve of the mad and the miserable.

Communities are surviving with the pain of loss, and the indignity of persistent Test defeats. They have not seen displayed on the field and beyond, an absence of pride and passion, and a daily diet of the ordinary as the new normal. The world that once marvelled at Windies excellence is now mesmerized by its mediocrity. Mystery and money exist side by side at the core of all explanatory models. No argument fits the bill or holds true for long. The reasons for the uprooting remain unclear. Cause and effect are tangled and mangled; more Tests are tossed.

The tale of the fall, unlike the rise, has summoned the mind of few academic writers. What survives on the surface, and suffices as obvious observations in the shallow, are easily discredited upon deeper reflection. But the offer to dig deeper, beneath the canopy of common conversations, is not without its attendant invective. The narrative that details the search for the soul that is sold is easily set aside in a highly charged emotional environment as an academic endeavour – meaning, in West Indian vernacular, fanciful and fictional.

Meanwhile, the high fever communities are running, has reached the Heads of Government who are demanding the restructuring of the CWI. Cricket, the state, and community are not in communion. There is a breakdown of faith, trust and belief in how best to imagine and pursue the fourth rising. But could the collapse have been prevented? The answer given here is a qualified yes. West Indians were drugged with their success, and sleepwalked into the nightmare that is loss of excellence.

But a deeper, more profound question is being asked. To what extent should the causes of decline be attributed to wider societal transformations? Cricket has long served as a barometer of cultural acumen and a thermometer of innovation and strategic action. Are West Indians, after 400 years of fighting for freedom from slavery and indenture, racism and colonialism, now an exhausted people? Can they get up, find new sources of fuel, reboot and rise to the top of the Test game for the fourth time?

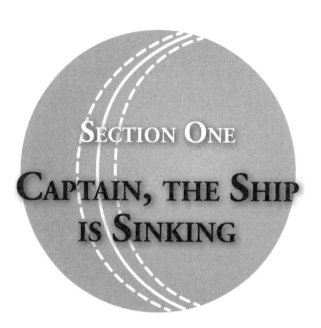

SECTION ONE

CAPTAIN, THE SHIP IS SINKING

1

TEN THEORIES OF DECLINE

Before the collapse, pundits preached of the folly and futility of cricket forecasts. As the crack grew larger, there was a frenzied call upon them for diagnoses and remedies. The diversity and elasticity of their responses stretched the imagination considerably beyond the boundary. Even within academia, there was no attempt at producing an integrated theory from the literary output. Each argument contained some modicum of truth.

The December 2015 edition of The *Economist* carried an editorial feature entitled 'West Indies Cricket: Gone with the Windies: Why a Dazzling Team Has Faded'. While for some readers it appeared unusual for a magazine dedicated to political economy discourses to focus on a cricket crisis in the Caribbean, editors undoubtedly understood that the financial and political fate and features of West Indian economy and society are tied intricately to the trajectory of cricket culture.[1]

The feature was illustrated by an image of a Windies cricketer in a fallen, undignified posture over the tagline 'Down and Out'. After recapping the statistics that contained proof of the collapse in the region's Test performance since 1995, the writer asserts that 'There is no shortage of theories to explain why West Indian cricket has declined so precipitously'. Readers are told that Windies 'golden age was unsustainable', and that 'some decline was probably inevitable'.[2]

The article sets out a number of plausible explanations, mixing internal and external forces into a cocktail of characterizations. There is no relative weighting of factors, but the writer insists that some wounds are 'self-inflicted' while others situate 'Globalization' as 'one culprit'. The evidence offered might require minor adjustments at the empirical edges. But the idea that 'with reform, Windies can arrest their fall' is not to be taken as a giveaway. Rather, it is to be read as an expression of confidence in the collective capacity of Caribbean people who had commonly demonstrated their ability to adapt to changed circumstances.[3]

Not surprising, as a financial forum, The *Economist* ends where its mandate begins – with the mantra that cash counts. 'Without more money,' it concludes, 'victories will be spaced', and as the 'international organization of the game militates against more money for the lowly – a negative business outlook for Windies is inevitable'.[4]

The attempts of experts and pundits to account for the fall of Windies produced an extensive discursively written and oral literature. To the extent that these diverse arguments and opinions can be grouped into analytical categories there are assembled and reformulated as general theories.

1. Natural Law: Rise and Fall

The idea that Windies would inevitably fall from the dominant position in international competitions has conceptual roots in the notion that what goes up must come down, a scientific law of earthly ecology. The emergence from a middle-ranking position in the early 1970s to global leadership by the early 1980s, and sustained for near two decades, is considered unnatural. No other cricket nation dominated twentieth-century international competitions in this fashion.

Dominance was the result of the forging of a formidable force that crushed opposing teams. Rivals were not just defeated. They were humiliated. Fear and trepidation were the common reactions to Windies rule. Careers of good cricketers were ruined, and teams ridiculed in front of their home communities. Regulations and rules were concocted by the International Cricket Council (ICC) in order to blunt the Windies edge. The dominance was defined by some officials as bad for the game; too complete for teams to compete.

A desire to see the end of Windies rule grew globally within the context of these official conversations. From the hearts of bureaucrats came a daily prayer for nature to complete what was initiated by rules and regulations – to level the playing field by flattening the Windies. But this route seemed rooted in fantasy rather than reality.

Nature, it seemed, was not a willing ally. Windies winning machine reproduced itself with increasing ferocity. The revised strategy called for a combination of natural laws and institutional rules. There was renewed confidence that such a merger would end the show and return Windies to a low ranking reflective of their physical size.

The call went out to the universe to reverse the historic eruption. There was confidence in the power of Councils and committees.

2. Globalization and Development Derailment

By the mid-1990s West Indian economies were in systemic decline within the context of galloping globalization. Most were trapped in structural adjustment programmes under the rules of the World Bank and the International Monetary Fund (IMF). The collapse of competitiveness and productivity in the face of larger economies and mega trading blocs had been obvious during the prior decade.

In 1995, when the Aussies defeated Windies in Jamaica, and took the Frank Worrell trophy, the island had not seen economic growth in 15 years and was in financial meltdown. Everywhere in the region there was sectorial unsustainability. West Indian economies were wilting long before the Windies team went down at Sabina.

The core consequence of structural adjustment programmes is the significant surrender by the state of responsibility for financing the social sector – primarily education, health, sport and culture. Working-class youth in particular no longer appeared a primary concern in public policy. The poor in general are removed from the policy front door. Economic stabilization and growth recovery strategies demand drastic cuts in public expenditure. The burden fell disproportionately on the poor.

Young, working-class men, cut off by the state, were left to fend for themselves. Youth unemployment increased as economic opportunities diminished. The youth spoke of state abandonment and class hostility. They took a fresh guard at the social crease and prepared politically to bat for themselves. Trapped in structural poverty, with no visible exit in sight, they imagined their society as an enemy.

The value system of traditional community cricket culture was first to feel the wind of change. The youth called for a detachment of sport from the scaffold of nation cricket, and urged to be seen as freelance professionals rather than public representatives. They demanded greater financial remuneration and focused less on issues relevant to public leadership.

The concept of the cricket hero, as a political construct of state craft and citizenship fell apart. Players expressed their freedom from tradition, and called on their employer, the West Indies Cricket Board (WICB), to contract them as global entrepreneurs and entertainers rather than community and state representatives.

Within this changed political and ideological context, Test cricket performance was starved of its energy source in nationalism and began to wither on the vine. Cricket heroes were replaced by cricket stars. The individual transcended the society and in the process came the end of passion for nation-cricket.

3. Retreat from Regional Unity

Economic decline across the Caribbean fostered the growth of political tension and conflict between governments. The commitment to regionalism as a prime construct seemed diminished, and was replaced by a benign form of non-ideological functional cooperation. While trade laws and policies reflected the growing insularity of regional communities, compromise on the commitment to the idealism of Caribbean oneness found fertile soil in the attitudes and decisions of citizens, cricketers in particular.

Windies cricket as a quintessential region project was designed to foster regional unity. It, therefore, felt with intensity the divisive forces of political fragmentation at all levels. The reduction of player cohesion in the locker room bred factions and fostered intra-team suspicion. This development resulted in player insularity with groups pulling in different directions, and sometimes all against the targeted captain.

In many instances players were assured that their respective 'home' governments would represent their attitudes and postures against selectors and other CWI officials. Political pressure mounted upon selectors, and officials were often expected to retreat and retract. Windies competitive power fell away resulting in low morale and further lack-lustre performances. The concept of 'political selections' to the team took root in the public imagination, undermining its internal social coherence and management. The concept of 'divided they fall' gained traction, and received popularity as an acceptable explanation.

4. External Destabilization

Dominant leaders generally generate, to their chagrin, a preference for the alternative, which serves to subvert and replace the status quo. The more powerful the leader the stronger these counter forces. Advocates of the 'alternative' often present their case in terms of the 'better interest' being served by restoring a prior reality or creating a future ideal. In a competitive circumstance, then, dominance generates anti-systemic forces that can reach virulence as they spread. Networks of opposition are spawned, dedicated to the fall of the leader.

Windies cricket was surrounded by external forces that sought to diminish and disrespect its achievement and contribution, and ultimately planned for its demise. The persistence of opposition found expression in official policies and places on a global scale. English cricket officials, especially, sought to suppress and remove the primal, emotional, cultural outpouring for Windies – the massive, mobilized, home-crowd support.

The Windies way was a peoples' path. It appealed to and empowered persons and communities that identified with the democratization it represented. Officials spoke of Windies 'noise factor', and set out to ban the entry to stands of drums and other musical instruments. They deemed the carnival expression of Windies cricket against the 'better interest' of the game, and refused fans the right to celebrate the brand in the stand.

Elitist elements within English officialdom sent shivers down the spine of their spectators who were galvanized to give thanks and praise to Windies players they identified as heroes. The bitterness of the assault upon the culture was palpable. Police searched fans for musical instruments, and public officials spoke of the 'hooliganism' of Windies fans. The joyful sound of democratic upliftment was defined by the mainstream media, willingly co-opted into the coup, as disruptive, distasteful and detrimental to cricket.

In addition to the hounding, there was the harassment. Fans were subjected to massive police presence in the stands, rationalized on the basis that potential criminals existed within their ranks. Armed police and their dogs dominated the perimeter and interior of stands and converted celebratory circumstances into a stage of State suppression. But there was no ethnic unity in the ugly intention to end Windies rule. English fans, in sections, stood with their heroes against the home grown heresy.

Where social harassment and political aggression failed, rules and regulation came to the fore. In boardrooms and back offices the primary targets were Windies fast bowlers. Officialdom understood all too well that speed was a main source of Windies force. Despite popular love and respect for the artistry and perfection of their craft, Windies pacers were defined as destroyers of the game, dangerous, deranged men with mean, menacing intentions. They were not superlative sportsmen, but sinister psychopaths using the noble game to give vent to their debased Caribbean instincts.

Cricket officials, and their media supporters, effectively turned the beauty of black speed craft into a cocktail of criticism designed to destroy men, morale and to vent their envy upon the Windies. Michael Holding, the most graceful of the group, was the prime target. He was named 'Whispering Death', a moniker associated with Windies rule and an approaching Armageddon.

The ICC passed laws to slow them down. A quota system was put in place to comfort batsmen who could not manage the short pitched delivery. In the West Indies, by contrast, the finest batsmen had defined the bouncer as a long-hop to be dispatched. The English defined it as a threat to their approved batting culture, and ultimately to national security. No more than one bouncer per over was legally allowed. Fast bowlers were demonized within the new regulatory regime.

The plan to cut Windies speed in the age of superfast computers was further implemented by setting a target for the number of overs to be bowled per day, and this at a time when five-day Tests against Windies were expected to end in three. The Marylebone Cricket Club (MCC) and the ICC went to work hand in glove against CWI. The 'men in grey suits' sought to restore supremacy to their 'boys with blue eyes', and to re-assign to them the long defeated right to rule.

The watching world knew that Windies were targeted by the power of rules, regulations, attitudes, and ultimately money. The *Economist* ended its review of Windies fall thus:

> Control of revenue from international cricket lies with the International Cricket Council (ICC). In 2014 the sport's three economic titans (India, England and Australia) forced through changes to the ICC that gave them more revenue than all other members combined. The result: the giants may soon have no one to play against but each other.[5]

5. Weak, Visionless Leadership

Effective leadership is a scarce commodity. It is not easily discovered neither can it be manufactured. It is that rare thing when thrown into the messy mix finds focus and surges above the surface. It is not readily created but it has the capacity to produce creativity. It transforms people and environments, and is recognized as the yeast that enables the dough to rise. Without it things fall flat. With it, flight, no matter how fleeting, is possible and pleasurable.

With the loss of the Frank Worrell Trophy to Australia at Sabina Park, Jamaica, in 1995, Richie Richardson's captaincy came under intense pressure. He was the leader under whose watch the ship was torpedoed. Australia, long a resolute rival, had struck a mortal blow in the heartland of Windies cricket before a crowd that included a weeping Michael Manley (no longer the Prime Minister) and a stunned Clive Lloyd. Out-maneuvered in a match that was balanced on a knife's edge – it rained heavily on the rest day – Windies could not hold on for a draw to tie the series and retain the trophy. From that moment the captaincy of Windies cricket became the most talked about and divisive subject in West Indian society.

Richardson received a rough rap. It followed him from Jamaica to England during the summer of '95 in which, despite a series win against England, team solidarity collapsed. Star batsman, Brian Lara, had walked out on the captain, team and management. He could not be found for a few mind-wrenching days. Wes Hall, the manager, Windies legend, and a recent reverend of religion, prayed to God for his speedy and safe return. He took to an evangelical church in Birmingham, just two miles away from Edgbaston – to call for divine intervention. When his prayer was answered, Hall gave thanks but knew that Richie's regime was not only tarnished but was effectively terminated.

Since then, the Windies Test team has languished in leadership purgatory. Choosing and removing captains seemed a game in its own right. Capped, and then decapitated, captains came and went as Test series were played and lost. The public praised each appointee on a Friday and nailed him to a cross on the Sunday. West Indians knew what they wanted, but it could not be found. They knew the qualities required but found no one to admire.

In West Indies cricket especially, leadership occupies a superordinate place. Oftentimes considered the most significant cultural leader in the politically fragmented region, the captain is expected to be a great unifier, the last hope to bring together communities God has put asunder. To be an effective Windies captain, then, is to defy God, by fashioning cohesion out of diffusion.

In this regard, only Sir Frank Worrell has been deified. Sir Gary, who first took Windies to the top of the Test world, after defeating England, India and Australia in succession in the mid-1960s, was uplifted and then pulled down when he lost the home series to England in 1968. Clive Lloyd, who took them back there, and kept them on top for near two decades, was normalized as only too human when he took his team into the Kerry Packer Cricket Circus in the late 1970s, against the dictate of WICB, and desire of half the public. Sir Viv, who never lost a Test series as captain, is still criticized in some quarters for his identification with the radical struggle for social justice, alignment with Rastafarianism, and advocacy of black ideology. Since the great Viv, the leadership space has been a desert storm.

After Richardson, Test captains have been a 'dime a dozen'. The 20 years between 1996 and 2016 have been tumultuous. There was Courtney Walsh (22 Tests – 6 won, 7 lost, 9 drawn); Brian Lara (47, 10, 26, 11); Jimmy Adams (15, 4, 8, 3); Carl Hooper (22, 4, 11, 7), Ridley Jacobs (2, 2, 0, 0); Shivnarine Chanderpaul (14, 1, 10, 3); Ramnaresh Sarwan (2, 0, 1, 1); Daren Ganga (2, 0, 2, 0); Floyd Reifer (2, 0, 2, 0); Darren Sammy (30, 8, 12, 10); and Denesh Ramdin (13, 4, 7, 2). Against this background, Jason Holder was asked to take the captaincy. In the 20 years before Richardson there were a mere four Test captains – Desmond Haynes, Viv Richards, Alvin Kallicharan and Clive Lloyd. The massive leap from a few to a festival is indicative of the deep, destabilizing crisis.

While these data speak more to the decline of team performance than the character of the captains themselves, the underlying assumption has lingered that defeat must be attributed to leadership incompetence. Fine cricketers all, and mostly men who in a talent-rich environment would have excelled and endured, experienced reputational harm within the paradigm that the captain must first be a natural 'leader of men'.

Immediately before and after the 2007 ODI World Cup in which Windies performed poorly, two Australians were appointed to coach the Test team. John Dyson was brought in following Bennett King's resignation. In short time, both men were hailed across the Caribbean and within the cricket fraternity for expressing what was already known that Windies needed an effective captain to lead the performance revival.

Sammy's appointment, for example, was explicitly an attempt to place the importance of leadership above the narrow confines of captaincy. When Floyd Reifer was appointed captain in 2009, following a strike by the Chris Gayle team on the eve of the home series against Bangladesh, official thinking moved to bring the intellectual aspects of leadership in line with the technical requirements of captaincy. Both Sammy and Reifer were known as players with passionate commitment to Windies cricket as a sociocultural force.

The 2015 appointment of Jason Holder is the ultimate declaration of belief in the power of the leadership principle. Just turned 24 years of age and with less than ten Tests on his testimonial, and yet to complete his undergraduate degree at the UWI, he is seen as the saviour of the post Reifer–Sammy leadership paradigm.

6. WICB/CWI Mismanagement

As Windies spiral into the basement of the Test monument they had built, all lips and eyes focused on the management – the WICB/CWI. The buck ends with the president, says the pundits, and from all quarters came the call to banish the Board. In the glory days, the experts have said, players performed to perfection despite the shortcomings of their employer, and were able to transcend industrial relations resentment as they racked up victories.

The charges against the then WICB are many and varied. Poor player selection policies and practices, inadequate player salaries and conditions of work, dismal marketing and financial leveraging of the Windies brand, undeveloped infrastructures for coaching and playing, persistent disregard for legends who were allegedly tossed aside as their productivity declined, lethargic legacy programmes to elevate and remunerate heroes, inadequate attention paid to youth development, indifference to public opinion, and critically, non-responsiveness to the early signs of decline. These criticisms and accusations were levied against successive presidents and boards who were held accountable for falling performance standards and horrendous employer-employee relations.

Critically, the then WICB, under President Rousseau, was accused of inaugurating the 'cash before country' consciousness. The board, critics said, abandoned its traditional non-governmental organization (NGO) image, and aggressively adopted the global corporate model and corresponding mentality. In giving effect to the mandate to secure the financial sustainability of Windies cricket, the Rousseau administration was criticized unfairly for selling the Windies' soul to sponsors while it excluded players, present and former, from the largesse.

The WICB was reinvented as a cash-driven organization that also unleashed player resentment and the 'each player for himself' approach to career development. Importantly, it led to the revival of the dormant West Indies Players' Association (WIPA) that was established in 1973. Responding to the Rousseau agenda, the WIPA was energized as an aggressive body demanding player participation in profits. It followed the path of the WICB, and was incorporated, in 2003, in Trinidad and Tobago. While respect for Rousseau's leadership grew, so did the contradiction that resulted from WICB's incorporation. He might have inadvertently promoted the explosion in player individualism that created the context for his humiliation by players on the eve of the South African tour in 1998 and his subsequent resignation.

WICB, then, has become the target for disgruntled men and women in the stand and beyond the boundary. It was believed to be in passive compliance with ICC's subversive tactics, and unwilling to stand up for players. At the end of each lost series, a call went out for the head of the president. In most instances, industrial disputes were settled by the public long before the president was given a chance to speak. Guilty was the verdict reached before the jury and judge had heard the case.

Before the 1990s, the typical Windies fan did not know the name of the president. Today, the vast majority can. In the 20 years between 1975 and 1995, there were four presidents – Jeffrey Stollmeyer, Allan Rae, Sir Clyde Walcott and Peter Short. In the 20 years between 1995 and 2015, there have been six – Patrick Rousseau, Sir Wesley Hall, Teddy Griffith, Kenneth Gordon, Sir Julian Hunte and Whycliffe 'Dave' Cameron.

In 2015, the cricket subcommittee of CARICOM reported that the Board should be disbanded immediately and replaced by an interim committee. Vocal elements within the public joined with Heads of Governments, calling for the President and Board to resign.[6] The *Economist*, in agreement with the critical Caribbean voice, stopped short of endorsing the call for the recall. It concluded:

> The WICB is guilty of self-inflicted wounds. In 2014 the Windies withdrew from a tour of India to protest lower salaries. Coaches routinely disagree with the WICB over the selection of players. And its Byzantine structure had made even a simple task, like scheduling matches, difficult.

The unacceptable nature of this circumstance fuels the public call to banish the Board. But it was not the Board that withdrew from the India tour; the players did – a big detail the public seemed willing to put aside.[7]

There is nothing like losing Test matches to light fires under leadership and management. Fans are feeling an intense pain which they wish to end. At the same time, they recognize that the politics of nationhood, in which players readily reject representing their country, preferring the more lucrative T20 global tournaments, does not augur well for the future. Yet, the first point of call in a storm is the first harbour. The CWI is considered the cause of the tempest and only its removal can restore the calm.

7. T20 Money and Mentality

Some hardcore critics have advocated banishing senior cricketers whose preference for the shortened T20 game over Test is overwhelmingly obvious. The T20 game is where most expect to find both gold and glory. They prefer the big, adoring crowds and the get rich in short games lifestyle that is filled with luxury hotels and media attention. There is no contest. Test cricket for many is the crazy option.

Windies superstars, and many emerging icons, wish to detach themselves from the rigor and robustness of the Test game. They have perfected the T20 in much the same way they mastered Tests and one day internationals in the glory years. Winning the 2012 and 2016 T20 ICC World Cups was a capping of their overall excellence.

Behind the victories, and the T20 preference of the team, however, are ideological and political issues that confront the West Indian public. The notion that West Indian youth are not psychologically equipped for the longer, concentration span of Tests, and as street boys have a short social horizon, is neither fair nor accurate.

It is far too easy to say that it is all about the money. The alleged loss of mental skill and toughness associated with preferences for 'short and fun' is not empirically supported. Their cognitive capacity to go the distance is said to be shot through, leaving behind the instant cash consciousness and gratification mentality of an alleged exhausted Caribbean culture. Critics refer to the T20 admiration as evidence of the lost generation; youth who are quick to draw the cash without delivering memorable, magnificent, performances. Fast food cricket, as some critics have called it, has taken over, and the youth care little for 'cuisine cricket'.

Accounting for the anxiety, the notion is that the T20 preference may be expressing in the main, the state of the nation, beyond the cash driven choices of cricketers. The idea that the development agenda of the region cannot be sustained by this consciousness disturbs policy thinkers. Furthermore, there is the perception that in the passion for the short game, resides a shocking loss of physical fitness and technical skills required to go the Test distance. The five hour jest is blamed for the diminished status of the five day Test.

The alleged loss of physical fitness, high performance skills, and techniques, the foundations upon which Windies cricket was built, is regarded as the logical, inevitable consequence of the T20 choice. Beyond the capacity to concentrate for multiple sessions at the crease is the argument that physical technique – form and shape – has been jettisoned for junk strokes and utter ugliness. If the Test game is seen as the pedigree horse to be admired, then the T20 bash for cash is the camel that gets the job done. It might not be an object of beauty, but like an ATM, it churns out the money.

The wholesale migration of senior players into the T20 bounty has produced disastrous Test results for Windies. The two approaches are seen as incompatible for a generation that cannot see long-term value in playing nation-cricket. Once the choice is made, the mind becomes committed to inflexibility. The youth, preferring the cash in hand, carry their gear to T20 with greater enthusiasm. This reality, say the critics, has killed and buried the Windies Test brand. The son, they say, has turned against the father. There is neither remorse nor shame. It is simply that the time has come for a new head in the household.

8. Inadequate Innovation: Poor Science and Technology Application

The advent of the digital age, in which science and technology are driven by innovation impulses, has found the West Indian world in the backwater of the global relations of Test cricket. While West Indians continue to dominate the Olympic track at the high speed end, long distance Test cricket culture has collapsed. Sport science and management, first class physical training, and education innovation in Windies cricket preparation lag behind the global competition.

The methods and techniques developed by Windies in the monument building era were adopted, innovated and applied by competitive teams. Since then, Windies appear fossilized and obsolete in most aspects of their operations. High-performance training techniques used by many countries are advanced versions of earlier Windies practices. The use in combination of super fit fast bowlers, for example, was a field technology perfected by Windies. It is now a global norm, and ironically, a force few Windies batsmen can effectively contain. Windies, then, are now bruised and battered by techniques they long ago invented.

This process speaks to the world of competitive cultural production. Innovation is more powerful, in the medium to long term, than invention. The English, Indians and Australians, especially, have innovated on Windies inventions. There is no patent to protect, and no property right to leverage.

The proof of the pudding is in the coaching. Windies responded by relying on foreign coaches to bring its Test players back to a globally competitive level. The third worldism of its Test cricket is seen on TV screens across the globe. It appears as if there is a lack of confidence and ability to command a competitive presence. The world now expects Windies inferior Test performances, humbled by technically superior foes.

Critically, there is no significant cricket equipment industry in the West Indies; bowling machines, bats, balls, paddings, computer software and assimilation exercises, as well as coaching certification and accreditation, are all imported and domesticated as the way things are. The science and technology gap became the rationale for preferring foreign coaches who were classified as accredited and certified, and therefore eligible. West Indian legends are required to enroll in Australian and English coaching programmes in order to be legitimized. The global ICC driven standard, that all coaches must be certified, placed 99 per cent of Windies legends in the category of 'illegitimate'.

The marginalization of Windies legends within global accreditation and professional training systems has created a major cultural problem for youth cricket in the region. Certified coaches have been asked to criticize Windies ways and adopt non-traditional techniques. The depth of this divide is not fully appreciated as a major return to psychological dependency. Windies cricket culture, then, has a counter-revolution to wage, one in which a return to self-confidence and self-validation are key components of cultural integrity.

9. Ramnarine's Rift: Legends vs Losers

The internecine war between the WICB and WIPA was fuelled by seismic fallout within the cricket fraternity between generations of 'legends and losers'. Fraternities are rarely known for perfect fellowship, but Windies cricket community appeared considerably more fractious than most. The flame was fanned by industrial relations conflict and media manipulation. It was both public and boardroom based. Legends and emerging icons squared off and even if unintended, a cold war ensued with occasional eruptions of heated exchange. On the outside it appeared that the generations were not generous to each other, fostering feelings of disrespect and sponsoring disunity.

CWI is constituted as a place where some legends hold power over young employees. The success achieved by the former is said to be surrendered by the latter, and doubt existed as to whether the legacy had been vigorously defended. Some legends have spoken of the sale of the family silver, while others have implied that carelessness, callousness, and lack of consciousness, resided at the centre of their defeats.

The result has been a cross-fire between generations. Their conflict resembled the washing of dirty whites in public. What should have been mutually empowering conversations turned into acerbic accusations and acrimony. It appeared ugly to the innocent and entertaining to the indifferent. The fraternity fractured, and education – the transfer of knowledge between elders and youngsters – failed to perform its task.

The absence of effective institutional relationships to harness the conversation illustrated the degree to which in the West Indies sustainability receives minimum investment. Shouting across the aisle and through the mass media take the place of round table dialogue. The fraternity did not appear in its best light during the years of Test decline.

The WIPA–WICB meltdown was an expression of the fundamental breach in education and professional communication. Suspicion and distrust hampered what should have been empathy, sympathy, and strategic planning. As the monument fell, Dinanath Ramnarine, CEO of WIPA, shed no tears and exuded no fears. Elders were told to move on and out!

Turned out from the house they built, the elders struck back! There was bloodletting in the public place, and shame descended upon the fraternity and community. The choice of the youth was to burn the house to the ground, or ignore the elder. Both options appeared on the agenda. Supporters of both sides lined up to fan the flame. As the Windies legacy lost its gloss, the lesson learnt remained clouded at the dawn of the new era.

10. De-skilled: Decentred

It is difficult to respect and fight for that which is inherited unless the inheritor is invested with an education that promotes respect, if not admiration. West Indian youths are less attached to Test cricket culture. It no longer fires their playing imagination.

How many times did they hear Sir Garfield 'Gary' Sobers say, that were he a youth today, golf would be his choice? Brian Lara has not made such a statement, but the alacrity with which he engages the game suggests an affinity to Sobers' declaration. Usain Bolt loves cricket, but chose track largely on account of parental pressure. What if he had followed Michael Holding and Courtney Walsh into the fast lane and became what Windies desperately need today?

Fantasy aside, there is more organized cricket being played in the region today than ever before. It is not a lack of capacity that haunts the culture. Rather, it is that the village academy, the community incubator in which Test excellence was conceived and delivered, is no longer an effective institution.

Cricket fields in remote villages that once fostered the skills of youth are now abandoned and left to grazing sheep. Trees that provided shade for village critics of youth technique and methods are now meeting places for a smoke and a drink. The village academy is closed in most places; the plumbing is broken in the basement.

The love of Test cricket was a road to salvation. Today, every youth knows that T20 cricket is the path to financial compensation. The youth are unlikely to stand tall and proud for their country and local team. Rather, they are likely to pursue personal accumulation by a skilful planning of an IPL debut, leaving behind incubator club and native land as inhibiting irritants.

The primary choice, then, is not between Test cricket and other games, but rather between heroism and stardom. The lessons of the Test legacy do not excite financially astute youth. The exuberance of uplifting the nation in Test series is secondary to the plunge into T20 luxury.

2

SIR GARY: TEARS OF A CLONE

Sir Garfield 'Gary' Sobers, the greatest of them all, Windies gift to humanity, was brought to tears in 2015 as the mission he masterminded 50 years earlier with his magnificent architectural genius crumbled before his eyes. Cloned and honed in the era of Worrell, Weekes and Walcott (the 3Ws), no one alive today can feel the depth of despair and agony the way he does. The penetrating pain tore the tears from his soul. Like Sir Wes Hall, Rohan Kanhai, Sir Conrad Hunte, Lance Gibbs, Collie Smith, and other siblings whose substance closely matched his own, Sobers had every reason to imagine that the pedigree line which sired him has ended.

The moment of his emotional meltdown and the place of his pain, were as personal as they were historical. It was in Sri Lanka, the country he had coached to confidence and that benefited most from his professional presence. In Colombo, Windies were taking on the host for the trophy named in his honour. He had an emotional stake in the success of both teams.

As Windies fell to the floor of Test rankings after another Test series defeat, settling just above Zimbabwe – the newest comer – his tears filled the television screen before a viewing world of a hundred million. 'My whole obligation was to West Indies cricket,' he said. 'I have never made a run for me.' Commenting on the absence of key senior players, who were otherwise engaged, he said: 'I have always played for the West Indies teams, and it was such a pleasure and joy to be able to do what I did. Records meant nothing; the team was important.'[1]

Unable to avoid the comparison with other Test teams, he spoke of the cash before country mentality which seems to be the ruin of his legacy. Playing for his country and comrades drove his quest to conquer. This was his source of energy, determination, and commitment to excellence. 'I don't think we have that kind of person today,' he said.

He continued:

> We might have them in different countries; we might have them in Sri Lanka; we might have them in England and in Australia, but I don't think we have that kind of person in West Indies anymore who is quite prepared to play and to give it everything to their country.

Then came the grand conclusion: 'That hurts, and until we can get people who are willing to play for West Indies in the right way, I think we're going to struggle for a long time. Other countries are going to come and surpass us.'[2]

T:1 Windies Test Series, 1980s

Season	Opposition	Victory
1980	England	1-0
1980/81	Pakistan	1-0
1980/81	England	2-0
1981/82	Australia	1-1
1982/83	India	2-0
1983/84	India	3-0
1983/84	Australia	3-0
1984	England	5-0
1984/85	Australia	3-1
1984/85	New Zealand	2-0
1985/86	England	5-0
1986/87	Pakistan	1-1
1986/87	New Zealand	1-1
1987/88	India	1-1
1987/88	Pakistan	1-1
1988	England	4-0
1988/89	Australia	3-1
1988/89	India	3-0
1989/90	England	2-1

At the time of Sobers' intervention Windies had fallen from first place in 1995, in Test and ODIs, to eighth position in both formats. Since 2012, they have not won a Test series against a higher ranking team. That was the year they defeated the struggling New Zealand team. The data detailing the decline speak to the greatest sporting catastrophe in modern history. It isn't simply about the loss of performance dominance, a circumstance that is common to all sporting enterprises. It is about the precipitous abandonment of excellence and fall to the lowest level.[3]

Between 1980 and 1995, Windies did not lose any of the 29 Test series they played. Following the 1995 defeat by Australia, the losses have been consistent and socially punishing. The public, said Viv Richards, looked to the team to bring some joy to their lives, but received instead persistent pain. Since June 2000, he said, they have won just 14 Test matches and lost 81 against the top eight countries, 'a record so miserable that the team's very survival is now in question'.[4]

Geoff Lawson, former Australian pacer who suffered at the hands of Windies batsmen, admitted, though grudgingly, that Windies men he encountered on the field were superior because they had 'skill and method in equal measure'. Also, he admitted, their bowling attack was 'majestic'. He paints a picture of Windies invincibility in the 1980s, and declared that their dominance was not good for the game.[5]

Lawson used the word 'brutal', for instance, to describe aspects of Windies tactics. For him the dominance was something just short of barbaric. He details a narrative of 'broken bones' suffered by Australian batsmen who were driven to wear protective helmet in order to save their lives. The 'barrage' of fast bowlers, he said, not only slowed batsmen's run rates, but in turn meant that 'over rates fell to single figures per hour'. The 'brutal brand of cricket,' he noted, 'forced the law makers to introduce over limits and a formal application of the intimidating bowling law.'[6]

The attempt to infantilize the once invincible team calls into being ideas about West Indian inability to solve their own problems. 'The great days of Windies cricket are now far distant,' Lawson concludes, 'and the chance of a new dynasty is exactly the same unless they seek and are given some outside help.'[7]

West Indians, according to Lawson, are incapable of devising effective self-help remedies. They lack both the reasoning and resources to rescue that which they love most, and for which they are respected. The collapse in Tests is, therefore, understood as an expression of societal decline in competence and cerebral capacity. Such anti-Windies sentiments run deep in the sub-text, and are embraced by many scribes, especially those former players whose careers were cut short or diminished by what had happened in their exposure to Windies. There is residual resentment and a need to ridicule Windies as a dying Test force.

If the official year of Windies decline is 1995, the shameful performance against South Africa by Lara's men in 1998 was certainly the beginning of the internal meltdown. All five Tests were lost after the team went on strike for better wages and conditions. It was their first Test tour of the country and the 'whitewash' received in the post-apartheid land struck like a meteor on the roof of every West Indian home. Windies had inflicted series 'black washes' in the past – India 1961 (5-0), and England 1984 (5-0). The chickens had come home to roost.

The ODI series was equally disastrous. Windies were shattered and shamed. It was the worst cricket performance, on and off the field, in their international history. The lowest level had been reached, and the greatest batsman in the world, Brian Lara, was at the helm. The dismal display was preceded by a series defeat by Pakistan during October to December, 1997. Three Test matches were played, and Pakistan hammered the Windies relentlessly. Pakistan won the first Test at Peshawar by an innings and 19 runs. The second Test at Rawalpindi, they won by an innings and 29 runs. The third Test at

Karachi, West Indies were again defeated, this time by ten wickets.

The tour to Pakistan was described as 'an unqualified disaster'. The Wisden Report recorded the graphic details of how 'the team's gradual decline from their previous high standards accelerated into free fall...losing all three Tests by embarrassingly wide margins.' It continued, 'Not since their first ever series, in England in 1928, had West Indies experienced such a thorough whitewash.' The team had lost its gloss, and there seemed to be no plan to restore the shine. The poor performance exposed the soulless team now characterized by 'inconsistency, indiscipline, and complacency'.[8]

Lara struggled. His 129 runs at an average of 21.50 indicated that his mind was not focused on Windies business. Walsh, the captain taking the castigation, did his heroic best despite reports that his team had internally collapsed on account of conflict between himself and Lara. The WICB did not name Lara as vice-captain for the tour, an expectation he had every right to hold on account of his previous appointment.

The batting 'plumbed new depth of ineptitude'. Batsmen were 'unable or unwilling to concentrate for long periods against a challenging attack in testing conditions'. The team, battered and bruised also lost all three of their matches scheduled in the quadrangular one-day tournament. On the whole, after their loss to Australia in 1995, their 'dreadful performances' in Pakistan confirmed that the Windies had lost the will to win.[9]

Windies arrived in Australia at the end of 2000. The writing was on the wall in bold letters. They went on to lose the Test series 5-0, a result that confirmed, according to Osman Samiuddin, 'beyond a shadow of doubt, that the West Indies were in the pits and that they would not rise thereafter.' They were splattered against the wall, losing two Tests by an innings, and one by a breathtaking total of 352 runs. Taking the tally, Windies had now lost a staggering six away Test series in a row. 'It was the last time they were considered good enough opponents to have five Tests in an Australian summer.'[10]

The previous year, when Australia toured the West Indies, the first Test at Port of Spain, March 5–8, 1999, had telegraphed much of what was to come. In the first innings, they were dismissed for a paltry 167 runs, but in the second inning the team miserably mustered a disgraceful 51. This was the outfit that arrived in Australia. The Aussies demanded reparations for the pain Windies had inflicted on them during the 1980s.

Three years earlier, the first sign was arguably the most spiritually gutting. Windies ran into Kenya in the 1996 World Cup, the team's first major international event. No one familiar with the basics of cricket history and culture could have imagined that Kenya could shame and disgrace the West Indies. They bowled out the Windies for 166 runs at Pune, and keeping their nerve dragged Windies over the coals for an agonizing 93 runs. After shaming Windies, the Kenyans ran all over the stadium in joyful celebration.[11]

Richie Richardson carried the disgrace that had been with him since Sabina Park. Martin Williamson noted that Windies leadership was in complete disarray. Richardson, he wrote, 'was under massive pressure to quit, and the consensus was that he was isolated and adrift from a side that no longer believed in him.' To add to the team's problems, the headline act, Brian Lara, 'at times seemed to want to be anywhere other than with the team.'[12]

Windies, Williamson suggested, 'were a shambles' going into the World Cup. The batsmen, he said, had become known for their 'fragile mindset', and even their best appeared out of it. Richardson is quoted as saying: 'I am the captain, but the players are also responsible; the whole setup is responsible; we're in a very, very deep hole; we're almost at the bottom.' Williamson quoted Michael Henderson of the *Times*: 'Their minds are elsewhere and they wish their bodies were. This was a disgraceful performance and the consequences will vibrate throughout the Caribbean for some time.'[13]

The Kenyans, decent to the dejected Windies, invited them to their changing room and told the press: 'West Indies are our idols and so to beat them is a dream.' Lara 'threw away his wicket like a spoilt child,' wrote Henderson. His was a 'pathetic and arrogant performance,' noted Peter Roebuck. 'This must be the depth for our cricket,' Colin Croft chimed in. 'I don't think we can sink lower than this,' Michael Holding concluded. Richardson, always stoic and statesmanlike in his manner, offered an apology to West Indian people: 'We're very, very sorry; we're as disappointed as you are. I have never felt this bad in all my life.' Six days later, he announced his retirement from international cricket.[14]

The collapse of Richardson's regime led to the appointment of the great fast bowler, Courtney Walsh, as captain, and coincided with the recognition of Australia as the world champions of Test Cricket. The 3-0 grubbing of the team by Pakistan, and the gruelling examination of the collapse by domestic pundits, facilitated the immediate replacement of Walsh by Brian Lara in 1998. Lara's leadership proved equally disastrous as the team plummeted even further into the doldrums of the Test game.

Lara led the team into the political quagmire of South Africa. He had called out his boys and thrown them into a power showdown with President of the WICB, Pat Rousseau. The industrial relations crisis on the eve of the historic tour soured the series at source and resulted in the post-apartheid white team whitewashing the Windies 5-0. He then led Windies into the 1999 World Cup, another disastrous engagement that led to their elimination in the group stages. The descent did not end. There was further to fall under Lara, the world's most brilliant batsman. He could not prevent the blading his team was to receive. Like the boy on the burning deck, he stood alone and aloof, as the team collapsed into shame and despair.

Then it was England, the ancestral enemy, striding confidently into Windies face. They were smelling blood spilt by the Aussies,

Pakistanis, South Africans and the Kenyans. It was dripping for the taking. And England, who for decades had not had the tenacity to attempt a taste, joined the line for their pint.

Five Tests were played in the summer of 2000. Windies won the first at Egbaston, but the result of the second Test was a declaration that they were about to be gutted. Bowling out Windies for 54 runs at Lords, England headquarters, the English came in line with the Aussies who had earlier ripped through them at Port of Spain for 51 runs. In the third Test at Headingly the English plot thickened; Windies were bowled out for 61 runs in their second innings.

England won the series 3-1, joining the pack that was picking Windies apart, tour by tour! Critically, the series win meant a grand reversal of England's fortune. It was the first time in 31 years they had won a series against Windies. At the end the tour, Curtly Ambrose retired from cricket, leaving the door wide open for those who wished to roast Windies rookies. The Wisden Trophy, like the Sir Frank Worrell Cup, departed Windies shelves for foreign lands, leaving the Caribbean cupboard bare.

Legend Clive Lloyd, who watched the slaughter, understood what it meant for Windies. He spoke of the capitulation of the team and the surrender of its dignity. It must not be 'dismissed as just another series,' he said. The Jimmy Adams team was substandard, the first to go down in England since 1969. The 'batting on this tour has been abysmal,' Lloyd added, and the store of 'youthful fast bowlers is bare. The entire Windies cricket setup has to be reviewed. We need to overhaul things from the top to bottom,' he concluded.[15]

Six months before Windies had reached England they were mauled by lowly New Zealand. When Lara's team arrived at Hamilton for the first Test in the first week in December, 1999, few experts expected that it could be defeated by 9 wickets. Neither did they imagine it would go down by a massive innings and 105 runs deficit in the second and final Test. But the worst was yet to come. Windies that had treated the Kiwis as practice partners for decades were whitewashed, 5-0 in the ODIs.

Lara fell on his sword and surrendered the captaincy. Michael Holding said the defeat showed a lack of spirit, a very painful affair, and Clive Lloyd reported that the WICB could call him anytime to stop the bleeding. The call did not come in a hurry. When the Kiwis made a return tour of the Windies two years later the bleeding had not ceased. Windies lost the Test series and New Zealand, the hitherto lowly islanders, surged above them in the Test rankings.

Jimmy's tenure went the way of Lara's. After losing to England 3-1, and whitewashed 5-0 by the Aussies, the WICB looking for new leadership in the broken dejected team, turned to the enigmatic Carl Hooper who led the team in 2000–2001 against South Africa. It was the first time, after a one-off Test match against the West Indies at Bridgetown in 1992 that the South Africa post-apartheid team was in the 'islands' for a full series. The political moment was massive in symbolism and expectation.

Windies lost the five Test series 2-1, and the ODIs 5-2. It was an historic achievement for the white Africans. Windies sunk even further into 'confusion and failure'. Hooper, too, had made his mark in history, becoming the fifth Windies captain in five years. His predecessor, Adams, was dropped from the team and sent into exile as the Sir Vivian Richard Trophy was flown to Pretoria.[16]

Hooper quickly followed Adams, and Lara was returned to the captaincy the following year. By then Windies were windless, having given up trophies to Australia, England, New Zealand, India, Pakistan and Sri Lanka. There was little left to salvage. Nothing was secure. Windies struck the bottom – the eighth place – ranked only above rookies Zimbabwe and Bangladesh. Finally, Bangladesh rose up and won four Tests against Windies.

Here, in this place, now resides the dearly departed, the once mighty men who took command of the world of Test. Twenty years of feasting have given way to 20 years of fasting. The drought shows no signs of an end, but all is not lost.

3

PASSING IMF TESTS: LOSING TEST MATCHES

In cricket, timing is everything. Like silence, it is golden and without it 'ducks' descend like rain upon the out of touch. By the 1990s, the nature of the interaction of popular political consciousness and Test cricket could not have produced worse results. It was the decade in which Caribbean development agenda ran into doubt, and political strategies were aligned with the thinking of the World Bank and the demands of the International Monetary Fund (IMF).

As economies entered a phase of systemic decline, so did Windies Test performance. National economies in the region reported worst case forecasts. Windies Test players fell deeper into the quality quagmire.

The 1970s and 1980s, in contrast, were a time of progressive political and social optimism, adventurism in the performance arts and culture, and confidence in economic strategies and development. The Caribbean reached beyond itself and looked to the world with a competitive certainty.[1]

The regional musical mind was magnificent. It infected the cricketers and their pride in the region poured out of their veins. Bob Marley was brilliant; Peter Tosh was turbulent; Third World was terrific; and Steel Pulse erupted from the English diaspora with pure passion. David Rudder and the Mighty Gabby celebrated cricketers with cause and purpose, representing their performance in tones steeled with determination. 'Get up, Stand up,' Bob said, 'Stand up for your right'! Tosh warned the 'downpressor man', and asked him 'where you gonna run to all along that day?' Gabby told batsmen to 'hit it! hit it in midwicket! hit it, hit it.' And they did.

These rhythms resonated with Viv Richards, the 'General', who as captain never lost a Test series war. The sounds of resilience and respect filled the souls of his warriors. He wore the colours of the Rastafari as an expression of this reasoning, and stood up as a leader of the cause, shoulder to shoulder, with Bob. He was the man of the moment whose mind was aligned to the season of optimism. He carried the hope and vision of the region with him onto the field.[2]

The decline came at the end of the first phase of the rejection of an oppressive colonialism that sought to cripple Windies creative and critical imagination. Jamaica led the way to Independence in 1962, followed shortly by Trinidad and Tobago, and Guyana and Barbados in 1966. The '70s and '80s witnessed the rise of the Leewards and Windwards. By the end of the '80s, most anti-colonial ships had sailed.

Driving the movement for the rejection of colonialism, and the assertion of independent states were political parties equipped with progressive ideologies that insisted upon citizens taking their rightful place in the palace of princes rather than the cane patches of plantations. Michael Manley was monumental in his erudition of the independence state of mind and the development of a politics of progress. He took up the lead from Eric Williams, Errol Barrow and Forbes Burnham – all men who believed in the potential of an integrated regional movement to take the people from poverty to prosperity.[3]

Manley had the benefit of the intellect of the quintessential policy thinker and practitioner, P.J. Patterson, a regionalist whose existential being was rooted in the powers of reason, resilience, and restitution. Manley told the region what needed to be done, and Patterson showed how it could and should be done. The maturity of the Caribbean enterprise was the visible sign of the time. There was eloquence and elegance, passion and pride and purpose rooted in the principles of progressive politics.

Politics, Culture, and Cricket were aligned in a fashion that fuelled each other, producing a fire that burnt the backward and illuminated the path for the progressive. Viv Richards led from the front with his bat and brains, and walked ahead of a battalion of bowlers whose flame brought not only fame to the team but also fellowship to his followers and to humanity.

Holding represented in his narrative the ideological line, and joined with Roberts to rip apart all opposition; Croft, Garner, Marshall, Bishop, Daniel, and Walsh came later to blow away the debris. The region was internally aligned and externally empowered. Citizens and state found respected representatives in cricketers who carried forth the concerns of the community.

Cricketer and state, then, spoke the same language, and believed in a shared vision. There was no conflict of consciousness in this collective leadership. Differences were diminished. Captains of Test matches were leaders of the public's right to participate in crafting the future of the region. The formula was fashioned as a trilateral-state, citizen and cricketer. It was the consensus of the Caribbean, and led on the field by conscious cricketers with deep ideological commitment.

By the beginning of the 1990s, neo-colonial political forces were ascending in the region. The defeat of the Manley regime and the violent implosion of the Grenada revolution sent a clear message through the region that social justice as a community objective was not the top political priority as economic decline ravished the meagre resources of the poor.

The regional shift in public policy in a direction away from community development to corporate accumulation was rationalized in terms of the urgent need for economic stability and growth. The political implication meant a turning away from working-class families that were now producing the majority of cricketers.

As economic decline accelerated in the early 1990s, and the region fell into the clutches of the IMF, the impact upon the poor was devastating. Resources required to support community programmes shrunk to nothingness, and youth cricketers, raised in a culture of poverty and facilities degradation, came to assimilate a perception of their political abandonment.

IMF programmes meant subjection of the region to passing of tests in order to quality to receive international fiscal and financial support. Passing IMF tests, then, became a top priority for parliaments while the poor were called upon to carry the disproportionate share of the material discipline that descended. Political governance under IMF testing has been torturous and torrid, demanding as it does the surrender of the poor to inflationary commodity markets. Structural adjustments of economies were imposed without flexibility. The overall effect was clear – the marginalization of the social sector and the poor, to achieve fiscal compliance.

As IMF rule romped through the region, a generation of West Indian youth came to maturity within a political environment that was characterized by state reduction of financial responsibility for community social development. Government cut back on traditional investments in public health, housing and education of the poor. With rising unemployment and increasing poverty came greater social and material deprivation in communities that were most productive of cricketing talent.

The vision of mass prosperity that had been framed by the progressive discourse during the 1970s and 1980s crumbled; two effects were the growth of rampant individualism and disrespect for the power and status of the state. Political parties, once seen as machines to spew out largesse to the lowly, were increasingly seen as the enemies of the underclasses. The public reputation of the state at the base took a beating. In communities most vulnerable to the vision of IMF, cricketers emerged with diminished inclinations to carry Windies flag.

Cricketers believed that there was a breach of the social contract that existed between themselves, the state and community. Respect for the functions of the state, at the base of society, is a crucial and necessary precondition for sustaining the sovereignty of nations. The community that was most productive in the creation of cricket talent was left to flounder as the price of flour, rice, and oil, burnt holes in their proletarian and peasant pockets.

The grassroots cricketers, then, were left to forage for themselves, and to imagine their interest in personal rather than public terms. Windies became a shattered window, unable to keep out the rain and ill-winds. Broken in the basement, and the plumbing leaking, society did not intensely focus on the need to rethink the social contract. Rising damp resulted, and in short time the entire edifice that once was the collective creation of state, society and cricketers cracked, and crumbled.

Cricketers found neither space nor sustenance in the new public policy parameters. The state surrendered the cricketer, and the cricketer in turn surrendered the state. The new anti-Test cricket consciousness found advocacy that corresponded with its survival concerns. Viv Richards rose from the pan-African sensibility, and Michael Holding hailed from halls long critical of deviant individualism. Fragmented collective consciousness followed each player into the Test arena. Without the grand vision they were visibly vulnerable to each commercial venture that appeared on the horizon.

This was not the world young cricketers wanted to idealize. They were prepared and willing to sustain the excellence inherited, but were politically unprepared by CWI for the task. Without public, political participation in framing a development discourse they distanced themselves from societal assumptions that they would eventually fall in, and be compliant. But IMF tests unleashed socio-economic forces that did not enhance youth mentoring. There were no WICB programmes to prepare them and to rescue the enterprise of their elders.

Windies, then, as a Test team, were sociologically subverted at source. They no longer shouldered the burden of the national purpose; the pain of defeat no longer crippled their mind; it became possible to party after the punishment. To laugh it off was to maintain sanity within the new reality. Cricketers gave back to society what they believed was handed to them – indifference and non-engagement.

Captain Richardson probably said it best when he unwittingly spoke about the first defeat at the hand of the post-apartheid South Africans. 'It was just another game,' he is alleged to have said. It was not the intention of the skipper to make light of the defeat by a team that had symbolized what West Indians had stood against for centuries – white supremacy. His statement resulted nonetheless in popular passions being inflamed precisely because citizens had heard what was confirmation of the new cricket ideology. 'Just another game' meant that pain would not haunt the locker room. If fans were prepared to torture their souls and spirits, it would not be so for the boys in maroon. Richardson was misunderstood, but the reported narrative resonated across the region as the new, official declaration of a defeated, diminished and dismantled Test culture.

More rattling of the heart of Windies supporters was the manner in which Captain Lara's public image evolved. Wearing caps indoors, hanging shirt tails, and unlaced shoes combined to create a presence that seemed inconsistent with cricket as a serious encounter. Lara became associated with the 'casual code'.

While the modern sporting personality had taken a twist from the formal to the fashionable, West Indian society was deeply divided with the dress code that was attached to the decline in decorum and determination. The 'cool' was back, but without runs and wickets; the hip sun shades and sun block filled the slips, but didn't strengthen them; high fives became more robust as successes became increasingly rare.

The symbols of youth masculinity served to mask the new mentality that reflected the IMF's notion of success. Test cricket is not a game for the rejected and dejected. It requires preparation for the long haul and is best played by minds manufactured in a movement of nationalist representation. It requires digging deep into the well that is the soul of the nation. To fight for a cause bigger than self, and is attached to one's identity as a member of a community, are the raison d'être of the Test culture.

The post-IMF Caribbean world can no longer produce the kind of mind at the grassroots that is willing to die at the crease in defence of community, and the common good. The 1990s' collapse of Test cricket performance is a direct descendant of the ascendency of these IMF-designed psychic affairs of the West Indian nation. To the extent that it has won the right to rule economies in the region, it is accepted but not respected. Its authority is rooted in the weakening of earlier efforts at sustainability and the flight from the historical legacies of colonialism.

Cricketers, especially those reared and raised in impoverished communities, struggle to excel in a climate where their communities are punished for the weakness of macroeconomic performances outside of their control. With the ending of Viv Richards as captain came a leadership paradigm that was devoid of political content and symbolism. It spoke to community advancement and national transformation around the concept of social justice. All good citizens of respected character, captains such as Courtney Walsh, Brian Lara, Carl Hooper, Jimmy Adams and Ramnaresh Sarwan, for example, were expected to rekindle development transformation first unleashed during the Worrell–Sobers era and found fertility during the Lloyd–Richard regimes.

IMF Testing, furthermore, created a distraction from the discourse that is the Caribbean self-reliant revolution that traditionally nurtured cricketers into becoming public representatives. The Test team today is formally representative, but it speaks glibly for the structurally adjusted, ideologically weakened, politically oppressed communities that do not know what tomorrow will hold. The T20 desire, on the other hand, is perfectly suited to this circumstance that leaves citizens to live from one IMF Test to another. Test cricket proficiency in the West Indies declined as IMF programmes became sublime.

4

NO MORE HEROES: STARS ONLY

The mid-1990s signalled the end of the Windies enigma and the death of two decades of dominance. Home tears flowed in the sunshine of Sabina Park in 1995 when the Sir Frank Worrell Trophy was handed over to Steve Waugh; discerning observers knew that a new mental construct was rising in the Windies. As the new sun was rising 'down under', it was evident to these observers that Windies were going down for the long nap.

Rain came in from the Blue Mountains on the rest day, but failed to shield Richie Richardson's team when play resumed. The team looked weak and tired, but there was more. The fighting spirit, long focused on the opposition had turned inward upon the team. The long civil war within the camp had begun.

It would be a war without a cause; no heroes to be held high, and no high philosophy to be upheld. Within the conflict resided an inescapable truth. Rampant individualism had gone wild; first and foremost an expression of the growing political disillusionment that typified the second post nationalist generation. Within the culture of performance, the emphasis shifted from the production of heroes to the generation of stars. The politics of players and their public commitment to community causes and consciousness gave way to the media images and commercial worth of stars. The hero was a player of the past; the rise of the star took centre stage.

The primary expression of the implosion of commitment to nationhood took the obvious form of player-employer conflict; verbalized in public acrimony in terms of the illegitimacy of CWI. Political leaders were called by many players to officially intervene, and some complied within the context of protecting cricket as a public good.

Title
Who Only Cricket Knows

To
Learie Constantine
and
W. G. Grace
for both of whom this book
hopes to right grave wrongs,
and, in so doing, extend our
too limited conceptions of
social history and of the fine
arts.

*Uncorrected Copy
but the essential
is here.*

*Cover Page of the original manuscript 'Who Only Cricket Knows' by CLR James,
published in 1963, as Beyond A Boundary, housed at the Centre for Cricket
Research, Cave Hill, The University of the West Indies*

Author (centre), presenting his book, A Nation Imagined: The First West Indies Test
Tour (England 1928) *to Prime Minister of Jamaica, Hon. P.J. Patterson (right) Sir
Wes Hall (left) 2006.*

Author with the sons and daughters of the legends of the 1928 West Indies Team, 2006

Author with Sir Everton Weekes, patron of University Cricket, at the 3Ws Oval, Cave Hill, Barbados, 2006

VCXI vs New Zealand (in foreground), Vice Chancellor McIntyre, Dr Luz Longworth and New Zealand Captain LK Germon, 1996.

Tim Hector, lecturing at UWI, Barbados, 2005

Author with Sir Gary Sobers, 3Ws Oval, UWI, Barbados, 2003

Launch of book in honour of Viv Richards (1996) UWI, Cave Hill. (L to R): Sir Everton Weekes, Sir Wes Hall, Tim Hector, Branford Taitt(M.P.) (editor, Hilary Beckles)

Launch of book of essays in honour of Sir Gary Sobers (L to R) : Leroy Parris, Sir Keith Hunte (UWI, Principal), Publisher, Ian Randle, Prime Minister of Barbados, Hon. Owen Arthur, 1994

'Blame the Board' became the rallying call. Under considerable public pressure, it developed an operational response suggesting that it was embattled; it dug in for a long resistance. Meanwhile, the world pondered why Windies found themselves in the veritable cul-de-sac.

West Indians are the only 'nation' in Test cricket that has since found itself unable to place its best team on the field of play. The team is often starved of the best talents, drained off by the lure of competing financial obligations and engagements. The team on the field is generally short of experience. The pundits are in agreement that the 2011/12 Test series against India, Australia and England, for example, all close finishes, could have gone Windies' way had the team benefited from the presence of the best players.

West Indians, furthermore, are the only Test cricketers who have successfully rejected Test duty. Other cricketing nations have made it clear to their citizens. To reject the team is to reject the nation. This is a policy position expressed in societies by political leaders, the media, the sponsoring private sector, and the general public. The principal political feature of West Indian society since the 1990s is best described in terms of citizens versus state. Citizens reject the right of the state to enforce public discipline in order to safeguard nationalist representation. Cricketers versus country became a primary political pastime; 'self versus society' is the energy behind the agenda.

The public, in large part, believes that cricketers should have the right to choose, and to make additional money whenever and wherever cricket is played. Some political leaders have said that the player should not be criticized for putting the nation on the back burner. The ideological weakness of the 'regional project' that binds the communities lies at the core of the crisis. The cricketer rejects the WICB, the regional agenda, and is often defended by national political leadership. 'Country before region' is the clarion call that brings forth 'cash before country' as players' strategy.

The academic community is divided but tilts in support of player liberty at the expense of team victory. This too, is a result of the growth of indifference to and doubt about the regional integration movement. As 'Island before region' rose within the politics, cricket became a primary reflection of what was beyond the boundary.

Through the gaze of the cricket craze, then, it is possible to see that West Indian regionalism is in deep trouble. Cricketers became frontline crusaders of a revived carnivalization of the West Indian mind that produced the 'we like it so' mentality – ironically a posture which our greatest calypso philosophers have urged us to avoid. The rampant market supremacy sensibility that urges giving way to unrestricted individualism informs cricketers' choices.

Beyond the West Indies, the cricketing world views the crisis in terms of governance out of control. The reliance on the IMF to instill order and discipline in a disenfranchised public is considered significant. Rebel cricketers rely on their 'home' community to protect them from regional opinion, and to seek legitimization in the critique of CWI as medieval.

So long as cricketers are empowered to reject the 'nation' in preference to marginal materialism, and be upheld in some quarters as heroes, Windies Test team will remain in the drain. The team goes into Test series without its vital stars. The global cricket community watches and sees this as a strange and unusual development.

While the freelancing of stars in T20 tournaments serves to entertain globally, fans everywhere now ask whether the Windies 'cash first virus' will infect their own team. Each Windies star has verbally expressed their love of team and country, but few are willing to choose the Test option. Instead, absence from selection is cleverly manipulated, sometimes medically, to achieve obvious exclusionary ends.

CWI, like all employers, has made errors in collegial management. Its reputation is now a low-hanging fruit, easily picked by every passing pundit not willing to think beyond critical media discourses even when fault lies elsewhere. Some saw the tsunami coming! They ran into the streets to warn the people, and wrote treatise about the coming flood. At the end of the 1990s when this literature began to appear there was no Indian Premier League (IPL); no Big Bash and no rejection of country for cash! The case was not compelling. Visionaries were dismissed as distorters.

The crisis in Test cricket performance is essentially a specific development in political governance and social disenchantment. The smoke generated by the heat has clouded the regional vision. The steam has blurred the focus and serves as a diversion from the real issue. 'Abolish the Board' has become the official call. Some women have called for an investigation into what seems like black masculinity gone mad.

Here, then, is the problem. Windies is the only Test team that is weakened chronically by the politics of economic decline. They are the only Test cricketers able to successfully reject Test match over T20 competitions. Australian officials have stated that no national player, if called to the Test team, could refuse representation and survive with respect in the nation. The Prime Minister, the media, the private sector and civic society would find the choice unacceptable; they would describe it a rejection of citizenship; an abandonment of the nation. The same political circumstance no doubt applies to England, South Africa, New Zealand and Pakistan. Such a player would be divested of house and happiness in India, and maybe a great deal more.

The thesis is bold. The global commercialization of cricket only subverted Windies Test cricket because in the West Indies the national resolve is unable to withstand its power. This is in part the result of a failure of CWI and political parties to celebrate and elevate cricket heroes in the aftermath of the Viv Richards–Michael Holding principled stance against apartheid. That was a leadership moment that saved the collective dignity of West Indians, and could have been the basis of a regional revival in cricket consciousness.

CWI is paying the price for what was really a political crisis that rests within the cradle of CARICOM. In 1998, long before the storm arrived, I stated that cricket heroes will…not wish to carry the burden of responsibility for nationalist pride, regional integration and the viability of the nation state. They see themselves as apolitical, transnational, global professionals, who desire to maximize financial earnings within attractive markets, and are motivated and guided by no other consideration. They consider the nation state as an oppressive rather than a liberating force towards which they feel suspicion rather than sentiment. The post-Richards generation, then, represents an unfettered economic individualism within cricket, a mentality that is consistent with the general policy and practice of the post-IMF supported nation states.[1]

Darren Sammy, as captain, was given a mandate to revive the heart and restore the soul of the Test enterprise. He was a mighty warrior confronting global forces with his Test team of brave young heroes. Initially, he was a leader charged with saying what each West Indian leader should say to cricketers: put your country first; play for your nation. Sammy was hailed a Worrell-like figure, leading a youthful Test team through the political debris. He was presented as a powerful mind; a gladiator of a rare kind.

After Sammy the desert closed in upon the dream that was once West Indian pride. As the city burnt, crowds danced to a tune played upon a steel pan. Until such time as Test cricketers are told firmly by political leaders and pundits that the operational philosophy is 'country before cash' and 'Windies first', citizens shall dream of glory, not in the future but in the distant past.

The Caribbean world, then, is in dire need of a development discourse that can assure its economic competitiveness and political sustainability as a viable civilization. The cricket crisis has provided the latest ground for testing the region's collective rationality and indigenous intelligence. These are bold statements, but then again West Indians have been boldest in the cricket arena.

Citizens are now poised, again, to outsource their last remaining global brand: cricket. They are doing so in much the same way that they have sold to the highest bidder their best commercial achievements, from beers to banks. They will discover within a decade that they were 'short changed' by ignorance of the enormous future value of what was sold. The buyers of these brands see what natives cannot. Financial value is drained away from the region in the medium to long term. Society remains impoverished even when the sellers are enriched by the exchange.

This is now the case with Windies cricket. Enormous political and public pressure is levied against CWI. It is urged to become a playing partner in what would clearly be the destruction of the pristine West Indian brand. The IPL franchises and other global buyers of Windies talent have no interest in the Test team as a regional construct. They have an interest in players as singular freelance entrepreneurs and are happy to support their detachment from CWI. They shake the Windies talent tree and the finest fruits fall to their franchises. This they know and expect because they know that the Windies brand is gold even though the branches are brittle. The commercial world knows the Caribbean fruit is both sweet and cheap.

The perception internationally that West Indian society is riddled with irrationality as evidenced in our political fragmentation and social contestations has exposed our best cricketers to the 'sign today and play away' culture. This commercial detachment has exposed social indiscipline at levels where it matters most; the idea of representing the nation. CWI, in this paradigm, is invited to become a minor part of the money-making machine for foreign dominant franchises. Their role is to produce young talent and release at random with no regard for the goose that lays the golden egg.

This is the true nature of the relationship between global franchises and West Indies cricket. It is best described as what the Chinese call a bacon and egg sandwich. One party to the deal brings the egg and the other party brings the bacon. But the pig must die in order to bring the bacon, while the chicken brings the egg and lives to reap the sweets of the deal. West Indies cricket is the bacon in the franchise sandwich; CWI is expected to be the bacon bringer.

CWI should be saluted for not going along with this arrangement and for standing its ground. Windies cricketers are not underpaid. They are easily in the elite of Caribbean skilled workers, earning millions of dollars within a five-year period. Their refusal to represent the region in its Test encounters should be placed within this context. There is no choice between poverty and riches but between riches and more riches; and between standing up for the region and walking away from it.

Windies Test stars are invited by international capital to become globetrotting entertainers; cash chasers who are cavalier with the legacy of excellence they have inherited from legends. While Test heroes from other countries hit the T20 road after serving their nations, our stars are engaged when Windies need them most. Yet, their expectation is that society must welcome them home as heroes, later in life, when the commercial pickings become slim and when they have lost the edge that did not serve at home. Herein lies the rub.

While CWI could have done more for legends, and for this failure is deserving of criticism, the same cannot be said of star players today. CWI is not the same institution of yesterday. The players who now reject the Windies Test team were created and nurtured by this WICB, and enriched by it.

A lesson from the cricket tale is that West Indians are confronted with having to externalize its development vision and drive. 'Let us all pack up our bags and leave our indigenous institutions to falter and hit rock bottom' seems to be an acceptable attitude and approach for many. To stand in the path of this perspective invites hostility and hubris. It's all the difference between one person's cash today and the community capital tomorrow. No Windies star called to the regional team should be allowed to walk away and play elsewhere without attracting a public political conversation that speaks to the subversive nature of such an action within the context of regional development. This is the straight ball often missed, or edged.

Recent comments from former captains about the role and function of leadership have provoked this reflection. Jimmy Adams spoke eloquently while offering his support to team solidarity. His intervention rests upon an image society holds of him; he is 'Jimmy the Gent', a social perception rooted in reason. Courtney Walsh also spoke in support. Everywhere the image of Captain Walsh is uniform; he is 'Ambassador Walsh'. These are interesting themes, forged in the imagination of the Caribbean public that scrutinizes actions and ideas, methods and manners.

Society has also settled, finally, its image of the legendary Shivnarine Chanderpaul. For a fleeting moment he was on the road to being more Saul than Paul, but after a trip to Delhi he paused, rediscovered his cause, and was canonized as St Paul, philosopher king of the crease, patron saint of stamina and the soul of sustainability. Ramnaresh Sarwan's sojourn as captain has been a flash in the pan, not long enough for image formation, but his semester in Leicester has reopened the discourse.

And finally, there is the now matured image of Sammy. In successive Test series, society came to see him as 'Sammy the Sampson', a Captain whose strength was seen, respected and celebrated. While George Headley had attracted the image of 'Atlas' for carrying the Windies on his back for near two decades after 1929, Sammy's enormous mental power and physical stamina have set him apart as the heroic leadership figure that dwarfed those he has succeeded.

It required no academic ammunition to theorize why in the first place Sammy was chosen for the role of leader. He was neither a star striker of the ball nor a bold bowler. His field performances were indeed nothing to shout loud about. But there was something else, more important at the moment, more valuable than Guyana gold, that was required. It was the mind of a leader within the context of West Indian development. Sammy's mind and mentality were more valuable than his runs or wickets. The ship needed a captain. Both the diligent and the negligent could see that it was a master stroke in strategic planning, an indigenous stroke, so to speak.

The heart and mind of Windies cricket were in need of rebuilding. The image of the captaincy and the intellectual values that supported it had fallen to such a low level that the generous in the world feared for the sustainability of the magnificent thing called Windies cricket. The decline of the development mind that had hitherto characterized the West Indies game, forged in the fires of the fight against colonialism, had resulted in the worst display imaginable. The team that once set world standards for professional performances became an assembly of under-performing, super cool dudes-stars, who transcended their states, but easily defeated in two of the five days allotted to a Test.

It was out of this depth of leadership despair, following the abandonment of ship on the Bangledesh tour that the Reifer–Sammy paradigm emerged. Floyd Reifer rose to the occasion and reconnected the image of the captaincy to its historic roots. Against Bangladesh and in South Africa, the contrast Reifer represented was striking. Sammy, his vice-captain, witnessed the wish for a return to sanity. He took over the reins and continued with the project of rebuilding the image of the captaincy, restoring the values of leadership, and reconnecting to the heart and mind of fans.

The decline was arrested. Sammy did not look back. He was a warrior for professionalism, ambassador for leadership, and the symbol of Windies strategic reaction to decline and despair. His presence was evidence that a mind was at work in the affairs of Windies cricket. It was a start to the counter-revolution.

Had C.L.R. James lived into the 1990s to experience these new features of Windies cricket, chances are he would have applied the dialectical method of Marxist political analysis and pronounced the end of the prestige of nation-cricket. Furthermore, he would have written about the re-colonization of West Indian economies by foreign multinational corporations and the loss of economic sovereignty in the age of globalization.

While players' financial incomes increased significantly in the Chris Gayle-era, winning Test performances decreased correspondingly. Most batsmen in the Test team have averages of less than 30, yet their million dollar annual incomes from T20 represent earnings ten times greater than Test players of ten years ago whose averages were twice as high at the peak of their careers.

Not surprisingly, there are frequent assertions that the Test team was populated by underperforming pariahs and 'show me the gold' pirates. The enduring hope is that the new mentality, connected to the earlier dispensation, will return bringing with it a familiar commitment to high performance, and broad-based leadership excellence.

The public continues to demand evidence of effort, and too often was outraged by a seemingly casual approach in defeat. It staunchly refuses to lower its standards in order to accommodate the generation of overpaid, mediocre players. Brian Lara is accused, often unfairly, of leaving behind a broken treasure not mended by the millions of dollars poured into the coffers of unprofessional players, some of whom, it should be said, have not been adequately prepared by CWI for international contests.

Lacking stamina, strategic vision, and rudderless for a decade at the captaincy level, the Test team drifted through assignments as if hoping for the odd good day. Cricket being ultimately a sport, does hand them the occasional good day, but more opportunities for victory were squandered on account of attitudinal ineptitude and professional indiscipline. In most cases, the flashes of brilliance displayed were followed by the glare of unbelievable incompetence and indifference.

Against the background of shifts in player attitude and beliefs systems, was the daily expression of aggressive industrial relations practices. The WICB did not dedicate sufficient resources to high-end management in order to chart and guide the modernization of the game. Critically, it has been unable to avoid the pitfalls placed in its paths by the new player culture that sees it as an enemy rather than ally.

The principal charge levied against CWI, however, did not emanate from players within the Lara–Gayle complex. Its roots go deeper into the mid-twentieth century. The argument has been made that the Board did not leverage the enormous influence of Windies cricket during its halcyon years in order to provide for the financial security of its heroes, and to develop professional support systems for the preparation of younger players.

Linked to this charge is the belief that players were left to scramble and scatter as hired workhorses in English county teams in the absence of a domestic professional competition. For decades, only players selected to represent Test and one day international (ODI) teams could make a competitive living playing cricket in the West Indies. The hundreds of players, who represented their individual countries, were not paid professionals. Most struggled to meet basic living costs during most of the year.

This circumstance ensured that young Windies cricketers were the most professionally and financially marginalized international cricketers. There was no significant sponsorship structure to support first class cricketers; and there were few meaningful opportunities for retired players to make a respectable living. Feeling financially insecure, and socially criticized, young cricketers sought to become globetrotters while pressing for more cash from CWI.

The legitimate demands of players were frequently received by cricket officials as part of a protest movement which served to further erode the possibility of joint corrective action. Mismanagement of the Windies brand contributed to the spawning of disgruntlement within the cricket fraternity, and the potential for performance enhancement was compromised by disabling industrial relations.

While earlier generations of Windies world beaters, and contemporary world losers, are united in common condemnation of CWI, they are divided by an acrimonious antipathy that serves to fracture the internal cricket dialogue. Heroes of the golden era, and young aspirants, see eye to eye on few issues. Generally, they have little to say to each other unless it is tinged with condemnation and invective.

Michael Holding summed up his group's thinking accurately when he indicated that Lara needed to have his head examined, a reference that spoke to his apparent indifference to the pain of elders following his second of three failing stints as captain. Captains Clive Lloyd and Viv Richards followed Holding with statements which suggested that Lara's team was not worthy to wear the 'maroon' colours of the West Indies.

With such strong words flowing from the lips of respected heroes, youngsters reacted with acidic tones that were far from respectful. Mutually assured destruction typifies inter-generational communications, and CWI seemed powerless to mediate. When former and current players assembled at official functions, each group held its corner. Like water and oil, they mingled, but did not mix; neither did they believe that it mattered. This crisis is best described as 'Legends vs. Losers'.

At the core of the crisis was something deeper, more profound. What it represented was a failure of the educational process since generations were not positioned to learn from each other. The successful transfer of critical knowledge that typified the relations between Worrell's team of the early 1960s, and that of Sobers' which followed, did not feature during the crisis decade of the 1990s.

Lara's main public ally was Sobers, the result of a mutual admiration that did not extend to his peer groups. Not surprisingly, Gayle had as his number one superstar supporter, none other than Lara, who celebrated his return to the leadership in the aftermath of the 2009 industrial relations crisis. In the face of no obvious options, cricket officials, pundits and experts waited with bated breath, hoping that Gayle and his team, rebranded 'Cool and the Gang', would somehow find the path to connect traditional standards.

Increasingly, however, there was growing evidence which suggested that the wait would not be in vain. The next generation – the teenagers in cricket teams – spoke a different language, seeing the cricket world in ways quite different from their seniors. Indeed, there is evidence to show media experts have argued that the Lara–Gayle legacy, and its relations to CWI, is fading as young players returned to the heroes of the Lloyd–Richard eras in search of inspiration.

Fans could hardly contain their excitement when young Adrian Barath, for example, on scoring his maiden Test century against Australia in December 2009, becoming the youngest West Indian Test centurion, made it clear in an emotional statement that he did not share the view that Windies Test cricket was a dying specie. For him the Test remained the truest, purest form of the game. Test cricket, he said, is where he wants to make his impact, and is the arena he most celebrates. His ambition as a Test player, he said, is to defend Windies brand. Sadly by 2012, Barath had vanished from view. Meanwhile, supporters journey to the past each time Kemar Roach, the pacer from Barbados, kissed Windies logo on taking a wicket.

It could be that two decades of public criticism of the Lara–Gayle leadership had its impact on the thinking of young cricketers who heard and saw all sides to the discourse. While they were attracted to the high incomes associated with the T20 game, and the glamour of lifestyles associated with Lara and Gayle, many have had mentoring opportunity and coaching support to realize that the 'nation' still provided ultimately the accolade of 'hero'. They marvelled at Sachin Tendulkar's respect throughout India, as well as Bret Lee's massive Australian fan base. Rebuilding the brand, then, seemed a logical and rational option.

5

THE EMPIRE STRIKES BACK: ENGLAND'S REVENGE

English cricket officialdom, in particular, took Windies dominance very badly indeed. They aggressively responded using all ammunition available. Not only on, but off the field – in the media and boardrooms, they struck. The assault was relentless.

First, the media attempted to discredit Windies success; second, officials used rules and regulations to subvert the team's performance; and third, counties excluded Windies elite cricketers from their professional circuits. Closing the domestic door on Windies elite cricketers was a backroom attempt to diminish their international status, and subvert the growth and development of emerging youth talent.

These strategies constitute an effective assault on Windies' best and respected. 'The Empire Strikes Back' became the metaphor of the moment. The covert campaign against Windies success was concentrated in England boardrooms and pubs where many players, officials, fans and media writers were less than polite in their choice of language. They took liberties with the reputations of Windies stars in a fashion unprecedented in the social history of cricket.

Michael Holding was precise when he stated: 'I wonder if any team in any sport has been subjected to such an orchestrated campaign of defamation as the West Indies has had to endure for so long.' Windies fans would celebrate exciting victories in the evening just to read mesmerizing media condemnation in the morning. Newspapers and magazines were maddening places for those who read for fair and objective reporting.[1]

Holding explained English hostility to enduring Windies success in terms of jealousy and their persistent defeats. He suggested it was 'a natural disappointment as England and Australia lose another series.' Aussie media counterparts joined the crusade. In some ways they were cruder in their critique, though less pseudo-intellectual and pretentious. But they were comforted in knowing that the financial and administrative power of the game resided in the Anglo–Aussie alliance.

Windies were caught between an Aussie rock and an English hard place. They had redefined the game on the field, raised the performance standards, filled the stands, empowered media moguls, but remained marginalized in the commercial and financial corridors.[2]

At the heart of the hysteria was an intention to unleash the hydra-anti-black racism. Michéle Savidge and Alastair McLellan, in their timely book, *Real Quick: A Celebration of the West Indies Pace Quartets*, published in 1995, captured the mood of the moment. They referenced the official 'belief that the game was being devalued' by Windies, and critically they recognized that 'jealousy and racism' resided at the core of the criticism.[3]

Media reports on Windies success were seldom balanced and analytical. They were generally accusative and specifically keen to deny the high qualities of players and their contributions to the international game. Importantly, they reacted negatively to Windies linking of their success to anti-colonialism and the struggle for racial justice.

The diminishing of Windies brand, in general, reflected the demise of the liberal art of English professional cricket writing and commentary, which the great and terribly missed John Arlott seemed to have taken with him beyond the boundary.

West Indies nationalism, some have said, more so than success cricket, has been the challenge for many English journalists, particularly as it has been associated with images and ideologies of black and Asian liberation. In much the same way that Windies cricket projected the flight of racially oppressed men and women from colonialism, England's cricket culture reflected the national urge to see them trapped perpetually within neo-imperialist thinking. English journalists, with few exceptions, when confronted with Windies triumphalism, easily retreated into the psychology of English imperial supremacy that oozed with condemnatory rhetoric.

Robin Marlar of the *Sunday Times*, and David Frith, editor of *Wisden Cricket Monthly*, led the charge against Windies. Not surprisingly, they focused with intense hostility upon the character and style of Viv Richards, who West Indians regarded as the proud symbol of their success and ideological icon of black liberation. Viv, the 'Master-blaster', became the target of their strategic assault upon the dominance of Windies cricket.[4]

Frith, who is widely regarded as an Establishment English voice, and a leader of anti-West Indian opinion, was quoted by *The Voice*, a London based black newspaper, as saying: 'Viv Richards is a sick man. He poisons the minds of black children and tells them to hate white people.' In a failed effort over several years to tarnish Richards' image as a progressive force in West Indies and world cricket, Frith succeeded in establishing a reputation for himself on both sides of the Atlantic as negrophobic, analytically weak, and culturally ethnocentric with a narrow grasp of cricket's enormous importance.[5]

In 1994, Robin Marlar, batting with Frith, stated that the West Indies 'game is founded on vengeance and violence and is fringed by arrogance.' After examining a decade of West Indies demolition of English teams, he surmised: 'It is my opinion that the current West Indies method, developed to perfection by Clive Lloyd, is deeply offensive to the essence of cricket, which is the defense of the stumps by a batsman rather than the defense of his own body.' In his opinion, West Indies fast bowling technology is in essence a reflection of Caribbean society where 'violence is commonplace'.[6]

The Australian team prior to the 1980s also had its periods of dominance, but was not perceived in England, or the West Indies, as 'overbearing'. England too had its period of ruling the roost which West Indian crowds and cricketers accepted in stride. But Windies rule, it seemed, 'offended their patronizing view of what West Indian cricket should be'.[7]

Furthermore, noted Savidge and McLellan, there was something 'more worrying' that motivated the criticism. The fact that the Caribbean side's success has been based on four 'big, black men' hurling hard objects at (mostly) white men was bound to inflame white supremacy consciousness, endemic to English society, and daily ventilated in corporate boardrooms and working men's clubs. In this world view, Savidge and McLellan noted, 'the West Indies side should be full of brilliant but flawed players.' But instead, it was populated by perfect professionals, an unbeatable proposition from natives who should be returned to a primitive place.[8]

'Pace like Fire' was the primary methodological breakthrough in Windies search for a competitive advantage. It was more a realization of truth than a visionary insight. In the 1975/76 series in Australia, Windies were put to the sword and demolished by the home-grown 'four pace attack'. The 5-1 grubbing received, detailed in reports of broken arms and bruised egos, was entirely due to the Aussie assault that featured four, sometimes five, fiercely fast bowlers. They wounded Windies pride but opened their eyes to the future.

There had been 'four pace attacks' throughout the history of Test Cricket, but the mid-'70s moment 'down under' added a new dimension. The speed bar was raised from 85 mph to near 100 mph, and a new age of speed was ushered. To survive meant to comply. Windies complied, competed, and soon took monopoly possession of the high speed zone. By 1978, Windies weapons gave them an advantage never before enjoyed or allowed to endure. They were not the innovators, but they did become the manufacturers. They held no patent rights, but their production and productivity were off the chart.

Meanwhile rage was brewing in the boardrooms as fear, jealousy and doom took root in opponents' changing rooms. How to undo Windies advantage became a global agenda. England led the way with methods its Empire had long perfected – negative attitudes, amendments to rules, and the unleashing of envy in every environment they administered.

S.Rajest has written eloquently and accurately about the reign of Windies speedsters. His in-depth essay on the 'amazing pace attack' sets the context for understanding the English reaction. At the outset, he said 'quite amazingly seven West Indian fast bowlers took 50-plus wickets at sub-25 averages' between April 1978 and November 1979. Furthermore, he added 'Marshall, Garner and Curtly Ambrose are the only three in the history of Test Cricket to take more than 200 wickets at averages of less than 21.'[9]

All opposing teams felt the power of this force and fell before it. Each fast bowler distinguished himself, setting records as the will of opposition resistance was broken. More than any other team, England seemed vulnerable and visionless. There were residual ideological issues of white supremacy associated with Empire, but the Aussies and India also carried racialized attitudes in their consciousness.

T:2 Windies Fast Bowlers Who Took More Than 50 Test Wickets, March 1976–February 1995[10]

Bowler	Test	Wickets	Avg.	Strike Rate
Ian Bishop	18	83	20.45	47.1
Malcolm Marshall	81	376	20.94	46.7
Joel Garner	58	259	20.97	50.8
Curtly Ambrose	50	224	21.11	54.2
Michael Holding	55	239	22.10	48.3
Colin Croft	27	125	23.30	49.3
Courtney Walsh	70	255	24.77	56.6
Winston Benjamin	17	52	26.09	59.8
Andy Roberts	34	133	26.78	58.1
Patrick Patterson	28	93	30.90	51.9

Britain continued to legitimize racial discrimination in both its global relations and domestic black community. Windies cricket, as an anti-racial culture, did its utmost to de-legitimize the racialized colonial legacy, and to offer a new, more enlightened, democratic path.

But importantly, Windies played more cricket against England in the '80s than any other Test nation. The 5-0 'blackwash' in 1985/86 Test series was a crescendo of sorts, a drama in which England experienced the deepest, purest pain in its cricketing history. The statistics of the beating England received at the hand of Holding and his cohort spoke the naked truth – that English batsmen were broken psychologically and appeared infantile in the face of the new speed regime.

In Test against England, Windies pacers took '88 wickets at 21.01 (1976); 85 at 20.24 (1988); 81 at 21.48 (1984); 81 at 25.27 (1980); and 81 at 25.26 (1991).' A few good players stood their ground. Graham Gooch, Robin Smith, Allan Lamb and David Gower were most resilient, but none was consistent and averaged less than 45 against Windies – 44.83, 44.69, 34.41, and 32.82 respectively. Only Sunil Gavaskar, the 'little master' of India, looked at home [without helmet], scoring 1135 runs in 15 Tests at an average of 45.40 with 5 centuries and 2 fifties.[11]

It was England that master-minded the political campaign to blunt the instrument they feared most. They did not resort to creativity at the crease, but used backhanded deals in boardrooms. The International Cricket Council (ICC) became known within Windies fan base as England's 'International Cricket Crusade'. The insider enterprise launched against Windies pace quartets was unforgiving and unrelenting. The focus of the crusade was to 'take away the most lethal weapon' of Windies. The 'West Indies pace quartet,' says Premachandram, had acquired in the 1980s 'a reputation for intimidating bowling', and so intense was the campaign against it that 'something had to give'.[12]

In 1991, the 'ICC introduced the "one bouncer per batsman per over" rule in an attempt to end the [Windies] intimidation.' The legislative lashing Windies received in the ICC assured England's batsmen who preferred to face the gentle medium pace and spin of earlier regimes. The pitch was rolled for the flattening of Windies. The ICC lost its credibility in the Caribbean for being the paid servant of England's racial agenda. 'It deliberately strangled the life out of Windies,' noted a respondent to Premachandram, 'by tailoring the rules to ensure "black washes" never happened again.'[13]

The obvious, odious anti-Windies ICC plot received widespread condemnation. The finest of Test umpires, Dickie Bird, described the rule as 'farcical', and argued that the umpire should be in charge of the game and its ethical rules, not doggy directors of the ICC Corporation. Bird called for an ending of the relentless attack on Windies pacers, and in so doing received the critical condemnation of his countrymen.[14]

When it was not venting about the danger of Windies pacers, England's ICC was expressing outrage about their alleged 'slow over rates' even when teams were blown away within three days in five day Test matches. It wasn't farcical, as Bird suggested, but fanatical. Sharda Ugra was on 'Line and Length' when he noted that the attack on Windies 'reign over the world' was an 'old world' surge to retain its hegemony that was taken away by the tall men from the New World.[15]

The temperature became unbearably hot in England during the winter of 1985/86, when its Test team received a 5-0 'black wash' in the West Indies. Losing by ten wickets in three days in the first Test at Sabina Park, largely at the hands of pacer Patrick Patterson, the team continued its downward slide losing the third Test at Bridgetown by an innings. By the time it reached Antigua for the final Test, which it lost by 240 runs, it was a broken vessel that made no sound. England's public media pressed for the nation to be avenged. Windies pacers were the first target, a low hanging fruit, ready for the picking.

Giving shape and form to England's outrage was Alastair McLellan's monograph, aptly entitled *The Enemy Within: The Impact of Overseas Players on English Cricket*. Published in 1994, it captured the animosity against Windies cricketers in English county teams, the fast bowlers especially, who were accused of pioneering the decline of the nation's cricket performance, particularly in the Test arena. The blame for England's lack of competitiveness was attributed almost exclusively to Windies. The pain, they said, was inflicted by Windies hand; it had to be cut off.[16]

The campaign to evict elite West Indian cricketers from the English county championship was the precursor to their punishment by the ICC with bowling restriction. English public opinion was formed around two concepts:

> That the West Indians had broken English resistance in the international arena because of their familiarity with English domestic cricket because they had been a part of it for near a century.

The English County circuit was the 'finishing school' for West Indian cricketers and had internationally launched most of their careers.

To end Windies regime, then, it was necessary to close the door on their youth talent, drive out seniors in the system, and classify all as the 'enemy within'. The strategy, they said, would give English youth an opportunity to grow without their confidence being ruined in their formative stage by the ferocity of the fellows from the 'islands'.

The 'kick out the culprits' school of thought gained ground during the late 1980s, and by the 1990s had become the common policy perspective across the counties. The Empire had struck back against the 'insurgents'. The proof was in the performance, said McLellan. 'England's declining performance at home', during the era of Windies rule, 'confirmed that competing against England in England is easier for those players who have come to terms with English conditions', ergo the Windies.[17]

By the end of the 1970s, the game in every English cricket club was to have a Windies pacer. The islands could not produce them fast enough. All through the 1980s, this trend continued. A Windies pacer gave the team a fearsome image, a focused competitiveness, and even if it was not the critical winning element, it assured the team a place at the top of the tournament table. McLellan noted that there was 'a rueful recognition of how English counties over the last decade [1980s]…sought to employ almost anybody hailing from the Caribbean who could, or said he could, bowl fast. The recruitment really took off after the West Indies' 1976 tour to England' when clubs and spectators saw for the first time the 'Windies' four-man attack in operation….Everybody wanted a piece of the action, and… most of the counties tried to secure a part of Windies' reflected glory, this time personified in the world's fastest bowler.'[18]

By 1990, the heroes had become the villains, and the counties, bowing under national pressure, aligned themselves with the 'good riddance' rhythm. From the 1970s, the Windies were the majority supplier of cricketers from overseas to the English counties. The legislation to limit the number each county could play was focused primarily on them. Critically, by excluding the West Indians the English were attempting to deploy the idea that it was an effective way to weaken Windies at the core by cutting off their emerging and elite players.

Windies selectors did treat English county series as a premier site for evaluating the available talent, and to sustain the supremacy of the senior team. Clive Lloyd's conquering teams, as well as Viv Richards's, were filled with seasoned English county players. The ideal Windies star, at home and abroad, was one who rose to elite county status, before being unleashed globally. To a considerable degree the county championship was their first global experience that provided exposure, not only to English players, but Indians, Pakistanis and Australians. Michael Manley was fond of saying the English county was indeed the West Indies Academy, a sort of finishing school.

Windies pacers were now defined as 'county killers', and more generously, 'bounty hunters'. The English moved to shut down the Windies 'county' academy, forcing Windies to fall back upon their own domestic base. It was a mortal blow to the body of Windies cricket, skilfully calculated and deployed. The bouncer was bowled by the Empire and the indigenous resistance was found wanting. Twenty years have passed and the signs of recovery from the amputation remain faint, distant and fragile.

When the news broke, for example, that Darren Bravo had signed a contract to play for Nottinghamshire County Cricket Club, Colin Croft, Windies pacer of the 1980s, was sufficiently struck by the implication to pen an article entitled 'West Indians Playing English County Cricket Are So Few!' Croft was aware that the pacers had been purged by the end of the 1990s when Windies were already in system decline. Bravo was a young, unproved batsman, an exception to the English exclusion agenda. He posed neither threat nor fear, but his selection was a surprise.[19]

T:3 West Indians in English Counties, 1980–95[21]

County	Players	Total
Derbyshire	M. Holding, I. Bishop	2
Essex	N. Phillips	1
Glamorgan	A. Cordle, E. Moseley, W.W. Davis, Viv Richards	4
Gloucestershire	J. Shepherd, C. Walsh, V. Greene	3
Hampshire	G. Greenidge, M. Marshall, E. Reifer, A. Roberts	4
Kent	J. Shepherd, E. Baptiste, T. Merrick, C. Hooper	4
Lancashire	C. Lloyd, C. Croft, B.P. Patterson	3
Leicestershire	Andy Roberts, G. Ferris, W. Benjamin	3
Middlesex	W. Daniel, D. Haynes	2
North Hampshire	R. Harper, W. Davis, C. Ambrose, E. Baptiste	4
Nottinghamshire	N. Nanan, F. Stephenson	2
Somerset	H. Moseley, Viv Richards, H. Gore	3
Surrey	S. Clarke, A. Gray	2
Sussex	F. Stephenson	1
Warwickshire	A. Kallicharan, T. Merrick	2
Worcestershire	V. Holder, H. Alleyne, R. Ellcock	3

Windies players, Croft concluded, are so few in the counties that 'these days one really has to look for the proverbial needles in a huge haystack. West Indian cricketers have long gone out of vogue'. Counties with 450 cricketers on their books, he said, less than 18 are West Indians compared to 20 years before when most countries had at least three, and many four.[20]

By 1995, the purge of Windies pacers was complete. While it has been said Windies Test decline is associated with the fall in quality rather than England's policy of exclusion, the players speak of the pain of performing in the racially charged county environment of the 1990s. Also, unlike earlier times, when emerging pacers were selected on promise, counties took less risk, slashed their investment in potentials and choked the careers of a generation of Windies cricketers.

As veterans of the 1980s county circuit moved into retirement, their successors could scarcely be found in the 'county academy'. This coincided with Windies changed image from invincibility to vulnerability. England won. Windies lost. The bleeding from the wound inflicted continues. Forced to rely on their dire domestic dollars to groom the next generation, Windies were exposed and deposed.

By 2000, England was ready to take on Windies in Test. In that year, they defeated them in a Series for the first time in 31 years. Three years later, in the 2003/4 series in the West Indies, they defeated them 3-0, and repeated the result in 2007 in England. In 2009, England continued to inflict the pain on Windies defeating the visitors 2-0.

The plan to supplant Windies was effectively executed over twenty years. The power of superior cash and administrative authority went bat in glove as England, with its allies, surrounded the wounded Windies and brought it to its knees. It was not all cricket!

SECTION TWO

SOUL FOR SALE

6

RISE OF COMPANY CRICKET: TEST DIVEST

It was 1995. The IMF was poised to breach the outer wall of the West Indian economy. No to currency devaluation was the public posture. The IMF wasn't playing cricket. They had no care for the game and the pride it represented. The wall stood proud and arrogant. 'The boys are back in town.' Barbados had finally joined the cohort of countries in the region which had been instructed to follow to the letter the conditionalities of the Fund's structural adjustment programmes.

In a sense, it was the beginning of a new West Indian postnationalist dispensation. Ironically, this notion of a new dispensation was the very concept used two years later to describe the ascendancy of Pat Rousseau, Jamaican entrepreneur, to the presidency of the West Indies Cricket Board of Control (WICBC).

The writing had been on another wall for Peter Short's presidency since the Sir Frank Worrell Trophy was handed over by him to the Aussies at Sabina Park in May 1995, and the Kenyan team knocked our heads against it during the World Cup a few months later. A new breed of corporate men – an aggressive elite group within the regional entrepreneurial community was trumpeting as public sector structures crumbled and fell into their private laps. The corporate boys were taking the town, and everything of worth that the structurally adjusted public had accumulated painfully over decades was made available for action – and cheaply – to merchants with a mandate masterminded by the IMF.

Peter Short was part of the respected nationalist network of civic society that believed in cricket as a cultural activity for community, part of the infrastructure of high moral values and social conduct. The IMF's effective control of the region's economy, its subjection of the national sovereignty of states to the financial interests of North Atlantic corporate hegemony, released forces through these societies that ran counter to traditional social and moral perspectives. The cricket culture represented by President Short was hopelessly vulnerable to the market economy principles being established under IMF–World Bank tutelage.

The cricket public could hardly be expected to ponder these developments, consumed as they were with the material devastation of currency devaluations, steep increases in mortgage interest rates, rapidly increasing working class unemployment, the shattering 'downsizing' of the middle class, and the spreading immediacy of an organized criminal subculture.

National economies were in crisis, and their primary public institutions, including cricket, were shaken to the foundations. These realities were global – at least in the South – and the crisis sent the chilling message throughout the West Indies that CWI, the last stronghold of cultural sovereignty was about to fall. An enlarged sense of economic desperation pervaded the region; everywhere citizens spoke of hopelessness and despair.

The strategic vision of IMF–World Bank thinking for the West Indies was the centering of the commercial mentality within all institutions. Governments were forced to 'privatize' public assets in an open market divestment programme that enabled wealthy elites to buy off, or buy in, what the national treasury had kept in trust for the people for some 30 years. Privatization became a metaphor for an immoral transfer of public wealth to private hands – from community to corporates. Public institutions, one by one, came under the new leadership of an empowered commercial class who had good reasons to believe that their time had finally come to control and manage the development process. They spoke of a new development paradigm; the failure of the traditional non-governmental and public sector, and the beginning of a modernized, corporatized society. CWI and UWI, noble institutions with global reputations, stood out like 'golden apples' against a tropical sky ready to be picked by the newly unfettered corporate force.

While it was recognized that the process of wealth accumulation and the expansion of market economies were important national objectives, there remained considerable doubt about the ability of this group, with a relatively unimpressive track record, to promote the level and quality of leadership required. But the crisis of economic accumulation somehow produced ideological effects that suppressed the effectiveness of these calls for caution.

Rousseau had made an impact upon the WICBC as chairman of the marketing committee. He succeeded Frantz Botek, another distinguished Jamaican, whose love for cricket and commitment to players had won him considerable admiration and respect throughout the cricket world. Botek, before his serious illness, had masterminded a strategy to extract considerable revenues from the global televising of West Indies cricket. Rousseau's project was to build upon this platform. As the financial needs of regional cricket boards increased, and players pressed for greater remuneration, the importance of revenue generation became the principal consideration of the WICBC. Indeed, the viability of West Indies cricket as an organized force on the world stage was threatened by the financial bankruptcy of the Board. It was altogether a most embarrassing circumstance, occurring as it did during the heyday of West Indian cricket leadership.

The discrediting of Richie Richardson's captaincy following the 1996 World Cup debacle, placed considerable pressure on Short's leadership of the WICBC. The way in which he handled the Brian Lara Affair of England during the summer of 1995 was used as the specific basis of a critique of his effectiveness. Short did not seek re-election, and the post of president was thrown open to contest. The weight of the financial argument could not be lightened and the

Board took the strategic decision to back Rousseau's nomination, despite considerable grumblings from former cricketers who saw him as driven by personal considerations rather than cricket development.

Peter Short, and before him Sir Clyde Walcott, represented the tradition of cricket as social art and popular culture, that did not centre the financial discourse. But the contradictions were clear to the world: the West Indies cricket team for 15 years was the world's strongest, yet its financial integrity was the world's weakest.

Rousseau was given a mandate to turn the mess into money, and to settle doubts about the financial viability of West Indies cricket. From the chairmanship of the marketing committee he was offered the presidency, ahead of well established veterans of the Board such as Alloy Lequay and Julian Hunte of Trinidad and Tobago, and the Windwards respectively.

Rousseau's reputation as an aggressive businessman stood him in good stead in Jamaica, though he remained an unknown factor in most Caribbean cricket fora. The successful globalization of West Indies cricket as a prime television commodity, his supporters suggested, required a person with his forceful corporate style to manage West Indies cricket. His detractors, however, suggested that while there could be no doubting the validity of this argument, they would prefer to situate Rousseau's business methods and skills in the marketing committee rather than the presidency. There remained, therefore, some unease about the interface of financial leadership and sociocultural representation. Capital and culture seemed polarized, calling for different kinds of mentalities.

The contradictory tendencies of globalization within the West Indies context became clear. Rousseau, to his credit, took the lead in forging links between local and international capital for the development of West Indies cricket, but his approach was received in some communities as hostile to the traditional, cultural and ideological integrity of the game.

Finding a sponsor for the 1997 regional competition became a top priority for the new Board. Cable and Wireless had already committed to a sponsorship of home Test tours for the remainder of the century. Rousseau had not declared a strategic vision for West Indies cricket outside of a marketing plan that involved selling the game to cable television stations in the US. No official statement was made about the obvious decline of community cricket, weaknesses in schools' cricket programmes, persistent gender inequality and institutional exclusion of women, and the destructive absence of a positive exit policy with respect to retiring Test players. A splendid and lavish banquet was organized successfully in Jamaica in honour of all Test players, but the public remained perturbed by the growing distance and level of conflict between itself and the Board.

Also, the public felt considerable anxiety about the social and educational role of cricket in the coming millennium, particularly with respect to its relationship to nationhood, cultural identity and the integration of these scattered but cosmologically unified communities. There remained the concern too that these discourses were not factored into the political economy thinking of Rousseau's leadership, as a result of the apparent alienation of the president from the ideological world within which Windies cricket came to dominance.

While the majority of working-class communities were especially supportive of the financial arrangements being made to reward cricketers, they remained disturbed by policies that resulted in their sense of exclusion, their loss of control, and the denial of centrality with respect to the reproduction of the cricket ethos.

The 1997 regional one-day tournament, modified, according to the press, along the conceptual lines of the American football Superbowl, was a typical example of these contradictory relations. The entire region was divided into two zones, Jamaica and Guyana, with semifinals and finals being held every year in Jamaica. This change in format had become necessary, new WICB marketing executive Chris Dehring told the region, because of difficulties being experienced by the WICB in securing sponsorship and in order to attract the North American market through satellite transmission of the games.

That Desnoes and Geddes took the opportunity to exploit Windies cricket in the promotion of its Red Stripe beer seemed to be the popular view. Effective sponsorships are generally those which suggest publicly, mutual benefit and respect. The arrangements of the Red Stripe Bowl from the perspective of cricket spectators seemed one-sided, crude and incomplete.

West Indies cricket, then, under Rousseau's lead, was subjected to a corporate agenda which reflected a slash upon its body politic in a way that no other previous sponsorship had done. Both the Sandals and Shell sponsorships in the past had not clashed with the internal social texture of West Indies cricket, neither had arrangements made with Cable & Wireless. In this regard, something new had developed, and insecurity and uncertainty became the dominant public sensations in relation to all sponsorship packages.

Writing in the *Daily Nation*, Andi Thornhill seemed more concerned with the alien nature of the marketing language used in the promotion of the Red Stripe Bowl. The opinion that Caribbean products need to be painted in American colours in order to be consumed by Americans, is clearly ill-conceived, though easily accepted. Thornhill asked, 'Has cultural penetration reached full circle, or is it a matter of reactionary marketing to make cricket more appealing to worldwide audiences?'[1]

The contradictory forces released by Rousseau's presidency surprised no one with an understanding of the Caribbean's experience with postcolonial market capitalism. The concept of 'global' is important here in that it illuminates the endemic nature of social tensions that arise from the interaction between the global and the local. As a concept, 'global' speaks to the process of emphasizing the critical importance of thinking globally but acting locally.

Rousseau's regime, then, alienated locals significantly in the search for a global (US) market.[2] In Barbados, Woody Richards described the entire enterprise of local alienation as 'A bowl of foolishness'[3] while Andi Thornhill's responses pointed out the conceptual 'cracks in the Bowl'.[4] Eddy Odingi, however, raised the 'red flag' and called to attention the underlying cultural crisis. 'We've to be careful,' he said, 'there is an element of dictatorship creeping into West Indies cricket and if we don't watch out, the unity which made West Indies rulers of the world for over a decade, will disintegrate. Not even the marketing skills of Pat Rousseau are worth that.'

The public spoke in one voice, and the Board recoiled to emerge with a promise to review the entire approach and operation. But the damage was done; confidence in the Board was shaken to the foundation; yet no one called for its removal. Memories of the Kingfisher sponsorship crisis had hardly receded before the public encountered the Red Stripe Bowl concept. Rousseau, who at the time of the Kingfisher crisis was chairman of the marketing committee, had placed his president, Peter Short, in a difficult position. Peter Short, in turn, went public with his criticism of Rousseau's presidency over the Red Stripe Bowl affair.

Tony Cozier, taking these and other confrontations between the Board and populace into consideration, summed up the first two years of the Rousseau regime as follows:

> West Indies cricket is in shambles. Utter, embarrassing and distressing… The responsibility for such a lamentable state of affairs lies squarely with the Board, the vaunted "New Dispensation" that was elected almost two years ago to specifically straighten out the mess that West Indies cricket was in then. Initially dynamic and innovative, it has now lost its way and is heading back into fallow territory, for so long the preserve of successive Boards.[5]

Cozier used as additional evidence the public ventilation of contest between the selectors and the Board over the captaincy of the Test team. When the selectors confirmed that Brian Lara had been nominated for the post for the 1997 tour of Pakistan, the media made much of his rejection by the Board in favour of Courtney Walsh.

Lara, in turn, publicly questioned the wisdom inherent in a system in which a board of bureaucrats could dismiss the decision of a panel of selectors made up of former Test stars. In all of this, the underlying issue, again, speaks to a contradictory tendency within West Indian cricket culture in the age of globalization.

Lara was undoubtedly the most globalized West Indian cricketer of his time. He was an international sport icon, recognized in the streets of all countries that share an English colonial legacy, which is some 70 per cent of the world's land space. Indeed, Lara achieved the global connectivity pursued by Rousseau in the area of finance. Yet, the evidence was clear that while Lara was expected to think global and act local, the Rousseau regime had fallen short of this principle. The overall effect was the display of contradictory tendencies at two levels of West Indies cricket, resulting from the crisis of national self-sufficiency.

The IMF's structural adjustment conditionalities were designed to produce resolutions to this crisis in which national sovereignty and sensibilities are seen as secondary circumstances. Civic society is understood as having no internal logic or legitimacy in itself, but as the supportive superstructure of the accumulation process in which the merchant mentality masquerades. The measurements of the Rousseau regime, then, were sanctioned by an imperial standard that knows precisely where its meridian lies.

Warwickshire made Lara their captain. But Warwickshire is a place long dominated by industrialists – people who make things and understand the values of production, productivity, national pride, and creativity. Birmingham, its leading community, is not dominated by merchants, people who sell things they do not understand how to make.

Rousseau did the right thing. He immediately dropped the word 'control' from the name of the Cricket Board, sending a signal that openness, dialogue, and indeed, democracy would characterize his administration. At the same time, he called for a united Board whose members should stand together on the critical decisions affecting the development of West Indies cricket. On the surface, it was possible to discern once again contradictory tendencies within these positions. At a deeper level, control remained a core objective, and continued to be while the discourses of civic society were not understood and respected as the energy sources of development.

For these reasons, then, certain aspects of the outcome of the Rousseau corporate revolution seemed predictable. The evidence was clear that the Board remained neither democratic nor open in its decision making, and this much had been confirmed by senior members. In October 1997, for example, chairman of the Board's development committee, Alloy Lequay of Trinidad and Tobago, stated during a press conference that 'cliquism' remained the dominant culture. He was reported as stating his intention of writing to President Rousseau 'pointing out to him that all is not well, that he does not have a united Board'.[6]

Furthermore, Lequay was reported as saying that 'what we are now recognizing is that certain critical decisions, which should be made by the Board, or by the executive, are being made by the hierarchy of the West Indies Board outside of meetings and not conforming to policy decisions. We are raising these issues,' concluded Lequay, 'in order to sensitize people that West Indies cricket administration is heading in the wrong direction.'[7]

Regarding the contest over the captaincy of the West Indies cricket team, Lequay was convinced that Rousseau's Board could be implicated, even if unwittingly, in a strategy, to which the media were principal participants, to 'put Brian Lara in a negative image' so as to diminish his standing with respect to appointment to the post. 'We have documentary evidence,' he asserted, 'that allows you to arrive at (this] irresistible conclusion.'[8] These very serious charges did not go unanswered by Rousseau, who was quoted as saying that 'maybe the plot is a figment of the imagination'.[9]

While the president's denial served to settle an aspect of this matter, it was received by the public as a signal that the Board was not at ease with a chairman under considerable public pressure and with divided and diminished support. Commenting on the effects of these contests on the public imagination, Tony Cozier also gave Rousseau good cause to reconsider the nature of his leadership methods. He stated:

> One of the first acts of the so-called 'new dispensation' of the West Indies Cricket Board was to drop the word 'control' from its title. Far from eliminating that C, it might have added a few more. Nothing has really changed and it remains the WICBC (the West Indies Cricket Board of Control, Controversy, Conflict, Confusion and Commotion). It fully lives up to its reputation, if not its new, abbreviated name.[10]

The Rousseau corporate revolution, then, represented more the emergence of a particular kind of policy than the triumph of a new vision of the development process. In effect, it constituted a form of institutional rationalization in that it signalled the completion of an alignment of West Indies cricket leadership to postmodern globalization. While Rousseau, like other institutional leaders seeking strategic global connectivities, had little room and less capital with which to manoeuvre, conceptual limitations engendered unnecessary social contests.

Since in most respects, Rousseau was essentially an 'old-fashioned' Caribbean corporate manager, a display of conceptual fidelity in reading the postmodern world can hardly be expected. The primary focus of his regime on the macro-financial dimension of the West Indies cricket predicament at the expense of its sociocultural infrastructure and ideological expectations, therefore, deepened the fracture between managers and the masses. The public preference was for an organic, interactive and mutually supportive encounter, rather than the subjection of the sociocultural to the corporate.

This crisis of management was essentially the outcome of a popular search for a new definition and mandate for West Indies cricket that respects and consolidates its historic culture and superordinate social importance. Differences between managers and masses with respect to the direction in which to find new meanings and methods for cricket clearly reflect the weaknesses of civic society and ambivalent attitudes to the corporate mind in the aftermath of the social reduction of the state.

Popular distrust for the leadership of the merchant class increased in proportion to the support it received from external financial institutions. The crisis of social trust and confidence in the region that deepened in the process of structural adjustment, located the Rousseau regime within the category of problem rather than solution.

Caribbean society continued to demonstrate its enduring opposition to an unchecked corporate mentality while at the same time yearning for the enlightenment of culturally uplifting and spiritually empowering ideas. The age of globalization magnified the intellectual dimension of this compelling, historic truth.

Rousseau's leadership did not enter a process of reflection and self-criticism. Much was expected of it and its potential for positive transformative action was considerable. What Rousseau had inherited, and the timing of his intervention, certainly complicated, if not prescribed, the parameters of his actions. There can be a genuinely new Caribbean way and method that emerges from a reading of Caribbean distinctiveness, simply because there is a recognizable Caribbean modernity. A cultural, rather than a corporate, revolution is required, that is, a radical, irretrievable break from the past that reflects the special, peculiar needs of Windies Test cricket in a globalizing age.

7

FROM 'WHISPERING DEATH' TO DOLLAR DIPLOMACY

Since the 'new normal' of poor Windies Test results individual players have never been richer. 'Big cash' flowed into the team as its rankings crashed. As Test was put to rest, the T20 train rolled into the heartland of the Windies game, bringing with it a fistful of cash in lieu of the bag of Test defeats.

No Windies cricketer has been as vocal about Test decline as legend, Michael Holding – dubbed in his dominant days 'Whispering Death (W.D.)'. W.D. was a comrade whose commitment to Windies cricket knew no boundaries. His desire to win was as strong as his insistence upon the dignity of being a maroon-clad warrior. Pride of purpose, commitment to learning and leading, W.D. was a symbol of the soul of Windies cricket at its pinnacle. There was never a possibility that his professionalism was within reach of corruption. Purity of purpose drove his passion. His mind was as focused as the ferocity of his deliveries.

To remember W.D. in his prime time is therefore to recall the character of Windies excellence and his political representation of his nation. As the man of the moment in 1976, against England to be precise, the world first grew to love and fear him. Windies had been whacked by the Aussies down under 5-1 during the prior Christmas and New Year. Beaten, spiritually bruised and battered into the ground, Clive Lloyd's young team arrived in the 'old Imperial centre' to be welcomed by a glorious summer and the greatest of insults from the captain of the country – Tony Greig. It was a defining departure in the political journey of Windies. Greig unleashed a verbal assault on the soul of the team that had recently been down on its knees.

Bred in the apartheid land that kept Nelson Mandela imprisoned upon an island, Greig declared to the media that the black boys from the islands would be hammered into the ground and made to kiss his feet. 'I will make them grovel,' said the South African turned Englishman. Slavery and apartheid, bonded together in Greig's consciousness, were to imprison Windies, as if on Robbins island.[1]

To witness the rise of W.D. to the moment that began Windies journey to the top was to understand why the soul is the salvation of the enterprise. Without it there can be no passion, a circumstance that allows for the ordinary to be ordained. W.D. was given a special task that could pave the way for a different future to unfold. His task was to target the man whose mind was identified as the keeper of the keys to the prison – and to bring him to his knees!

Lloyd, the chief strategy leader, had seen the inner strength of this remarkable 22-year-old youth and entrusted him with the mission to do the impossible. As Greig came to the crease, Lloyd called up his asset with one objective in mind – to send the mendicant and his mentality back to the pavilion. The plan could have backfired. A project so daring, placed in soft hands and a young mind, was truly a test. Holding took the longest run, and with perfect balance, exploded his Caribbean consciousness in a fashion so sophisticated few have understood.

Never before in the history of Windies cricket, except maybe when George 'maas' Headley took on the Aussies in '33, and Sobers in '57, had a mere youth, like the Jewish David, been tasked with taking on a Goliath. As Greig came so did he go! Holding didn't allow him to linger. He came like an English train, on time, and departed in minutes, as expected. No theatre in the towns of England had seen such high drama.

Windies stood up, dusted off their soiled whites, and rose to a new height. Holding held aloft the soul of the emerging team, and gave it a new sense of its possibilities. There was no language in England appropriate to describe the intellectual and spiritual power of Holding, the heretic. English was inadequate, and Jamaican a tad too colourful. His words were a West Indian syncretic form, heard in all the communities of the Caribbean and understood perfectly because of his pitch, tone and diction.

Greig also heard the sound, but it echoes in his 'ego' like the hiss of a snake. What he heard was the noise of the ball passing between bat and pad. Then there was the thud of leather on timber and the loud cries of joy. At the end of the mission, the youngster had taken 28 wickets at an average of 12.71 and a strike rate of 34.1, the best performance of the seminal series.

W.D. was the youngest member of the team. With a brain filled with political ideas and cultural consciousness, he symbolized the spirit of the rising Caribbean identity and the soul of Windies cricket project. From this youth came the power of purpose and the passion for performance. His alignment of attitude and energy created the force that was the brand of Windies. This is the legacy he is now asked to witness, dismantled and destroyed by minds not made up to represent Windies.

As the 2015 ODI Cup marched on into Australia, Holding now an icon in the commentary booth, could only plead with Windies batsmen to concentrate on the business at hand. The players, he insisted, are simply not 'thinking about their cricket'. One by one, he said, they are just 'reckless', demonstrating in each match 'irresponsible batting'. Chris Gayle, he noted, clearly the team's match winner, 'just throws his bat at the ball, losing his composure and just swinging because he has got so accustomed to the shorter form' of the game. The entire team shows a 'lack of commitment, lack of thinking,' he said, 'just going out and playing instead of thinking about what they're actually doing.'[2]

For two decades Windies fans had been calling for greater commitment to the legacy, and showing performance respect for the standards established. Writers, media professionals, and the fans in the stands have cried out for application and loyalty. The players and the public have been at odds over the absence of professional passion and quality performance. Crowds have said that the care factor within the Test team is too low, and that the loyalty level almost obsolete.

While 'cash before country' has become the philosophy, officials at CWI have been calling incessantly for its reversal, and have declared the 'nation first principle' to guide selection policy. Michael Muirhead, CEO of CWI, on December 19, 2015 reiterated the eligibility policy by emphasizing that each player must show commitment to the regional competition in order to be eligible to represent Windies in international tournaments. This proclamation came in the aftermath of the publicly declared player preference for cash-cricket on the global circuit. Windies' best players are not yielding to the policy framework of WICB bosses, and each year make their preferences clear. The clash of causes has meant that CWI, for over a decade, has not been able to put the best Test team on the field.

The philosophical conflict between player and employer has racked Windies. Participation politics is generally understood by observing publics in terms of rightful players resisting a vengeful Board, when in fact the issue is commitment to team versus the individualization of market choices. Most players do not have access to good financial data and some are short of relevant skills. The result has been that Windies cricket culture is typified by a crude and inelegant dialogue in the media that pits the quick cash option against the representation implicit in Test cricket.

All cricketers within the global sport arena are faced with the same predicaments and choices. Each player seeks to maximize personal financial income and social outcomes. They are exposed to the same range of reason that reflects the game as public representation and private accumulation.

Two conclusions can be drawn from what has been seen thus far. First, Windies cricketers are amongst the least effective in the management of the choice. They are the only players who publicly and aggressively confront community social sensibilities by running roughshod over the domestic claim. They alone openly reject the national call, and receive considerable public support.

Second, West Indian economies, the smallest and most vulnerable in the Test cricket space, offer players the least financial remuneration for their skills. The inability, or refusal, of the wealth ownership and management sector to embrace elite players at the level of international expectation has been the basis of players' rationalization of the rejection of the nation in favour of the private franchise.

The argument frequently made by players is that they are expected to take 'status' to the supermarket to buy steak. This represents, to some extent a distortion, but the unsuspecting public is willing to accept its validity and implications. The sum of it all is that the Test team has emerged in the twenty-first century as 'unfit for purpose'. Test selectors are expected to run through a list of the available – those remaining after the Indian Premier League (IPL), Big Bash, and other festivals, have creamed off the top.

The reduction of the selection process from a focus on the 'eligible best' to the 'available rest' is a metaphor that sends the message as to why Windies cricket creeps along the floor of each Test tour. The WICB's ability to enforce eligibility rules is sometimes weakened by political pressures. When a senior player breaches these rules by choosing Big Bash or IPL over Test and domestic competitions, he calls upon his prime minister and the mass media for support. Thereafter, empowered by politics, he expects to 'walk into the team'. Selectors have tried to ignore the infamy as political pressure mounts.

The contrast with what obtained earlier is striking and symbolic. The image of the 'four horsemen of the apocalypse' as the first Windies pace quartets that ruled the world was called – Roberts, Holding, Croft and Garner – is one that represented Windies plurality coming as they did from Antigua, Jamaica, Guyana, and Barbados, respectively. The region worked as one, a powerful force of diversity; each element drawing strength from and for the other; each a part of the whole. They recognized that differences in community origins were real, but celebrated their interdependence and the power of solidarity.

Curtly Ambrose, the next generation horseman, joined his mentor, Michael Holding, and spoke of the need to reaffirm the principle of 'nation first' in selection policy. 'No player', says Ambrose, is more important than the team. The persistent preference for the IPL over Windies Test, and the 2014 Indian Tour walk out, came against the background of the Chris Gayle led strike in July–August, 2009, that resulted in the unavailability of the 'best team' to engage Bangladesh. The tour was completed with the 'best available team' led by Floyd Reifer. Bangladesh 'white washed' the replacements 2-0 in Tests, and 3-0 in one day internationals (ODIs). The original squad comprised Chris Gayle (Captain), Denesh Ramdin (Vice Captain) and Dwayne Bravo.[3]

Lloyd's mandate as Chairman of Selectors was to restore order in this aspect of Windies' affairs, and to validate the traditional values that had made the Test team strong and the performance culture sustainable. Senior players who appeared most vocal in support of the India tour walk out were left out of the 2015 World Cup in Australia. The logical consequence of rejecting Windies was their isolation from automatic re-entry. This seemed reasonable and in the best interest of the game and nation. 'We want to move on,' Lloyd said, and 'we want to move on with a new captain.' Critically, 'we want to reward people for the way they have played.'[4]

Players who participated in the leadership of the 'walk out' were not known for 'exceptional performances'. 'We really and truly want to pick people on what they have done for our cricket and not anything else. We have looked at all of that,' Lloyd said. When asked about the impact of the 'walk out' he said:

It hurt because that (tour) was part of the building process. We were trying to get a good Test side to play against India and then we would have been better prepared for South Africa and at the same time, we would have got the World Cup squad that we wanted. But all that was disrupted and we had to start rebuilding against the best team in the world. It is very difficult…I am talking about our top-class players – their averages are not that good in all types of cricket.[5]

Lloyd also drew a direct parallel between the performance mediocrity of players and their capacity for disruption. The public reading of this connection has been that the low-value added of these players should not give them the capacity to inflict maximum negative outcomes. He concluded his assessment by saying:

We want players interested in West Indies cricket and make sure West Indies cricket is important. West Indies cricket is important to me. It has given me my upward mobility…We don't want to stop you going to different parts to earn money, but you must be ready for us wherever we have our cricket. And I don't see that as difficult.[6]

That is, he called for that which is currently unpopular: a counter-revolution in Windies cricket.

In this regard, Lloyd has had the full backing of some legends who speak simultaneously to the reality of individual choice and the imperative of rebuilding Windies Test cricket. For him the 'Windies first policy' has to be respected as the standard. This policy is found in action in all competitive cricket nations. 'Unfortunately,' he says, 'some of our top players are in IPL' and are rarely available for the home team. 'You can't really stop someone, or you shouldn't stop someone from making decisions. They have got to decide if they want to play for the West Indies or go to the IPL. I know it is a lucrative thing [but] should we just allow these guys to come straight back into the team? For me, I think not.'[7]

Sir Gary took an assessment of this circumstance to a logical conclusion. He expressed fear for the long-term future of Windies Test capacity. 'In the 1980s and 1990s, West Indies were champions for about 15 years,' he said, but 'I don't think you'll see that again in the history of cricket. High profile cricketers such as Chris Gayle, Dwayne Bravo, Kieron Pollard and Sunil Narine have deserted their international side and opted for T20 franchises.' He concedes, nonetheless, that cricketers from 'humble backgrounds' will continue to place cash before country.[8]

Other Test playing countries have had a different experience. It is not true that Windies players are significantly underpaid to represent their countries. Indeed, their contract income is generally competitive with other Test-playing countries. It is also true that their poor performances relative to other countries has created an anomaly; as their income increases as their performances fall.

Sir Gary, however, does not accept that 'poor family' context is an acceptable explanation for rejecting Test duties. Players, he insists, 'should be able to use discretion and understand the difference' between national duty and personal freedom. In so far that he does not believe players will exercise discretion, he acknowledges that the T20 global circuit will 'be affecting West Indies more than any other nation'. His analysis ends with the grand assertion that 'T20 leagues across the globe have destroyed West Indies Test cricket.'[9]

The decline of Windies Test, as imagined by the 'King of Legends', is a prescription based on the lack of commitment to the cause and culture of Caribbean society. From the highly ideologically charged circumstance of Holding to the dominant individualism of the current cohort, the decline is best explained in the context of an absence of an organized social movement within the second phase of the nation-building project.

The 1970s and 1980s constituted the period in which Caribbean youth joined nationalist movements dedicated to social justice, ethnic equality and condemnation of the financial greed of elites. These movements were essentially part of a political process in which the masses stood against the continuing legacies of neocolonialism and white supremacy at home and abroad. It was a call for social justice within the context of nation-building, and a confirmation of the values of political solidarity, expression of cultural identity rooted in the African and Asian sensibility that had facilitated the flight from slavery, indenture and colonialism.

Bravo led the Windies off an ongoing Test tour in India because of an industrial dispute with the West Indies Players' Association (WIPA), bringing the region's cricket to its knees in the face of a concerned world. Yet, he seemed surprised when his captaincy was taken away, and his selection blocked in the subsequent World Cup. The persistence of his narrative of personal victimization in the aftermath of his abandonment of responsibility to team, country and global sport, is as phenomenal as his inability to understand what he had done. Again, what was displayed within the Windies environment is the tragic, undeveloped political nature of leading cricketers, a circumstance that prevents their comprehension of complexity and ability to make effective choices.

Despite his open conflict with the WIPA, Bravo was responsible for his actions that weakened Windies reputation. The limits of his thinking found expression in the dismay at being disciplined. He did not believe there should be accountability for his private actions in respect of the public culture that is cricket. The lack of accountability in his attitude permeates his personal practice of the public culture. The political articulation of his views says that the nation and state are subordinate to the individual, and that his philosophy of representation is rhetorical rather than real.

The standoff between Windies cricketers and the WICB, on the 'nation first' selection principle, should surprise no one with an interest in post-colonial political governance in the Caribbean. Youth culture, in critical parts, is seeking to establish dominance in public governance regarding the political processes. Political leaders are also pressed to devalue the importance of managing public institutions. CWI, largely on account of its own inertia and ongoing, intense bombardment with player revolt, sponsorship shortfalls, marketing pushbacks and international institutional unfriendliness is seen as socially vulnerable even if legally impregnable.

The players, then, struck with a view to taking administrative control of Windies cricket and to craft the new dispensation in their own image. The WIPA's agenda under Dinanath Ramnarine was to take over the operations of Windies cricket, replace CWI, and operate international cricket as an industry dedicated to personal financial empowerment of a few with no regard to the legacy of excellence, and the role of the sport in regional development. Ramnarine's project was to control the financial aspects of the global brand, and establish a management clique around the income and its status.

It is within this context, then, that the agenda to de-link and depoliticize cricket can be understood. Bravo articulated his position by stating that Windies must move with the changing times. It isn't that Bravo is blind to his own role in weakening the future of Windies Test. He does not see his personal record as poor, given the leadership position he held as a senior player. As a batsman, to date, he has played 40 Test, and in 71 innings scored 2,200 runs at an average of 31.42. In 164 ODIs, he has averaged 25.36. His bowling has been equally unimpressive; 86 Test wickets at an average of 39.83 and 199 ODI wicket at 29.51.

The fans understand all too well that the current cohort of IPL icons, Gayle excluded, did not perform satisfactorily for Windies in Test and ODIs. The Test team continued its losing ways with them, which weakens considerably their claim of CWI victimization. This was the basis of the argument by coach, Otis Gibson, who in the review of the 2011 International Cricket Council (ICC), ODI World Cup performances expressed disappointment that the senior players had all tragically underperformed. When Gibson spoke of their comparison with players in other teams, and presented the statistics, Windies top players took him to task as divisive and overtly critical.

The most consistent aspect of Windies ODI World Cup performance was its collapse for low scores despite the availability of IPL stars. Scuttled out in the semis against Pakistan on March

23 for a measly 112 in 43.3 overs, and going down by ten wickets meant the end of the World Cup for a team that had not won a game against a higher-ranked competitor in more than two years.[10]

Chris Gayle, Ramnaresh Sarwan and Shivnarine Chanderpaul, all failed miserably while players of similar experience in other teams performed thrice as well. Ottis Gibson opened the discussion, suggesting that senior players were failing on account of poor fitness and sub-par applications, and that maybe it was better not to 'pin hopes on some of those senior guys', and 'move on and get some youngsters in. A lot of our players,' the coach said, 'need only to look at someone like Sachin Tendulkar. He's the sort of senior statesman in the Indian team, but he also seems to be the hungriest guy of the lot. He gets runs almost every time he goes out to bat and India can rely on him. We need to be able to rely on our people the way India rely on him.'[11]

Not surprisingly, Gibson's truth was responded to by vitriol from senior, failed players, as well as their apologists. The team had lost 19 successive matches against leading teams with senior players who 'threw away game winning positions against England and India' Chris Gayle managed just 170 runs in the tournament, Chanderpaul 114, Sarwan 115 and Kieron Pollard 180.[12]

Four years later Brian Lara arrived at the same conclusion as coach Gibson. He called upon the selectors to 'discard the current generation and bring in [a] fresh set of players who can play the sport with passion'. This cohort, the master player contended, not only lack passion for Windies cricket but they also 'lack the understanding of their cricketing history'. They should be 'shown the exit door' because they are more inclined towards 'lucrative Twenty 20 leagues' rather than playing for their nation.[13]

This choice to play Test for Windies was exercised over a decade by senior players. When they were occasionally available, their performances were persistently poor and damaging. Their presence was associated with added 'stress' within the camp for everyone –

coaches, managers and selectors, and there was always the greater risk of an industrial relations action leading to a withdrawal of enthusiasm or a walk-out. When they were unavailable, a public relations campaign to legitimize their choice spiralled beyond the boundary.

The decline of Windies Test cricket, then, has many facets, but central to the damaged nerve centre is what the public sees as the betrayal of the legacy, retreat from performance excellence and the selling of the soul of the team. Betrayal is viewed by some critics as too harsh a concept, suggesting as it does a conscious, coordinated effort. But the Caribbean public, and diaspora communities beyond, on assessing the evidence of a decade of commitment withdrawals, walk-outs, and sub-par performances, have good reasons to arrive at this conclusion. The explosion of personal financial interests in the IPL and the implosion of the culture of excellence in Test have produced the matrix of mediocre outcomes.

The upward journey to excellence between 1976 and 1996, and the descent into the decade of despair after 2006 are reflected starkly in the statistics. The richer Windies players became in the decades after 1996, the more ragged their Test performance results. Cash, it seemed, had corroded skill sets, eroded fitness and corrupted their community consciousness. The nation demanded respect from those it called representatives. As performances plummeted, and shame fell upon the citizen, cricketers cashed in.

8

ROUSSEAU'S REBELS: THE TOUR THAT SOLD THE SOUL

November 1998 will forever be etched in the annals of West Indies cricket as the moment in which it faced and failed its greatest political test. It was the time of Windies first official tour of the post-apartheid republic under the presidency of the great liberator, Nelson Mandela. The players, led by Brian Lara, with Carl Hooper as his vice captain, created in the world of Pan-African affairs a seminal crisis. It was the historic tour in which the soul of Windies cricket was devalued and sold.

Windies went on strike for more cash in the face of the emotional, spiritually anticipating, welcoming president. The wounded icon, named Madiba by the masses, did his best to rescue Windies from the political meltdown. Long known as a great fan of the Windies brand, now host to his heroes, he suffered a seismic setback that tore into his soul. Not even his personal plea could get Windies players on the plane.

The tour was symbolic for those millions of Africans who had paid the greatest human price in their effort to overthrow the criminal white supremacy regime. It was intended to bring Windies liberation cricket into the emerging democracy with a view to building an alliance for the betterment of humanity.

Windies players, not understanding or caring about this compelling context, took a stand and said 'no cash no cricket'. Observers with political imagination and historical awareness did not see this coming. How could Windies players especially have discounted the value of celebrating Mandela's presidency, and offering solidarity with the youth of Soweto and others? It was an act of political backwardness perpetrated upon the liberation legacy of Windies cricket and the consciousness of great heroes who had worn maroon.

Since the beginning of the decline in 1995, it was the test the Windies could least afford to fail. West Indians, and their official cricket, had turned their backs on the apartheid evil in Southern Africa from the moment in 1948 the regime of 'white first' was officially declared. In the same year, Windies hero 'Maas' Headley – Jamaican mother, Bajan father, Panama born and Jamaican bred – became the first black man to be appointed a Windies Test captain. As apartheid rose in South African cricket, it fell in West Indies cricket.

All efforts to legitimize the inhumanity of apartheid were rejected by the Caribbean community. The public and their elected leaders stood on point and poured scorn upon the scourge imposed upon African people by the racist, criminal colonialists. West Indian communities stood resolute, unflinching, in permanent hostility to the infamy. Cricketers played their part, and those few who fled there in the 1980s to sell their skills for a fist full of rand were rejected, isolated and branded as pirates and pariahs. They were officially branded 'rebel cricketers', the few who did so much damage to so many.

Windies icons stood in opposition to white supremacy and provided the world with legendary leadership. Captain Clive Lloyd issued a warning that any member of his team who crossed over into the tortured country would be unwelcomed back into the fold which he considered a moral force. Michael Holding felt insulted that apartheid officials could invite him as a proud African Jamaican to sell his birth right for a 'mess of pottage'. Sir Viv Richards, like Michael the lion heart, was offered a rash of rand to put his soul on sale. He told them that their gold was not good enough!

Fifteen years later, President Mandela was at the helm of the liberated country and was ready to officially receive Windies. It was an historic moment in the bloody history of a nation now on the move and ready to give thanks to those who had stood on its right side. Windies were top of the list. This was it; the celebrated Windies were to visit and be a part of the recognition of the president.

Before the ink could dry on the president's invitation, news of a pay dispute between Lara's men and President Rousseau's Board took to the streets. There was a clash for more cash that would 'leave West Indies cricket in the gutter.'[1] In the West Indies there were reports that the darkest clouds were circling over its cricket; concerned citizens felt numbed and crippled.

The team was expected to arrive in Johannesburg on September 5–6. The core of it had completed a one-day series against Bangladesh and was on its way to South Africa via Bangkok. It was there, as the plane stopped to refuel, that the crisis took final form. Lara reportedly held conversations with tour manager, Clive Lloyd, who sent the message to CWI in Antigua. The extra cash demanded was not approved nor released by officials, and as a consequence, team members refused to take the connection flight to Mandela land, but detoured to London until the funds were found.

The disbelief at CWI reflected the general feeling across the Caribbean, and the Pan-African world. This was more than the sabotage of a series; it was the greatest insult to the new nation and its respected leader. The Caribbean that had cared and fought for the liberation movement was confronted by its cricketers who had hitherto made it proud. President Rousseau, showing righteous indignation, fired both Captain Lara and Vice-Captain Hooper. He deemed them both unfit for Windies leadership.

The two players took the president's fire power as a powder puff, and effectively ignored his power to call the shots over the future of the tour. It was a declaration of war between players and president. An effort to replace the dismissed leadership had failed, as player solidarity stood in the way of instructions from headquarters. Members of the team issued expressions of solidarity with their discarded leaders, and called for action to unite the full team in

London. Lara and Hooper, no longer officially in charge of the team, also received full support from the West Indies Players' Association (WIPA).

The clash over cash had its impact on all sides of the divide. South Africa cricket officials, led by Ali Bacher, was fearful of losing considerable international respect, and domestic revenue, if the tour was abandoned, while the team took a stance – no extra cash, no cricket! In the Caribbean the concern that the team had messed with the mind of Madiba generated rage. The great president, an ancient fan of Windies, deserved the respect and the hospitality of the team; this was the sentiment and language on the streets. That the strike was wrong, plain and simple, was the summary in every Caribbean community. Soweto was outraged!

South African officials played their last card to get the cricket out on the grass. No amount of talking could get them out of London's Excelsior Hotel where they were marooned. President Rousseau summoned them to headquarters for a meeting, but the message he received in return was clear; if you want to speak with us, you know where we can be found! Rousseau, having lost control of the ball game, rushed to London to meet his rebels.

Ali Bacher, and his colleagues, also rushed to London to meet the rebels. The content of Rousseau's hand luggage was not known, but Bacher was carrying a letter addressed to the cricketers from President Mandela pleading with them to end the standoff, and to tour as his guests. The President of the liberated country was reduced to a begging posture, news of which further enraged West Indian society at both the levels of political leadership and grass roots.

The 'madness against Mandela' was too much for many Windies fans to bear. Neither Walsh nor Joel Garner, WIPA representatives, could succeed where Lloyd had failed. Despite the letter from Mandela, there was no breaking news. The players continued their standoff, leaving Bacher to sweat, and Rousseau to ponder his power as president and employer. Day three into the dispute, the global media were growing impatient with the incredible inflexibility of the Windies captain and team.

When news eventually surfaced that players would fly out to South Africa, there was no longer a Windies team in the performance sense of the term. Despite their claim that the team had genuine concerns, not only about fees and emoluments, but about security, the believability of their statements was universally belittled. The team won the dollar battle and went on to lose all five Test matches and six one day internationals (ODIs).

The soul of Windies had been placed on the bargaining table in London. In the scheme of things, Mandela's letter did not turn the deal, but the dollars Rousseau promised the players. There was no team because each member, cash aside, knew that they had degraded Windies brand and placed their nation in a very dark place. The *Daily Nation* of Barbados reported: 'The lessons of the last week, was an experience which might well have led to the death of the spirit of West Indian cricket at the highest level.'[2]

The team looked defeated and embarrassed before they entered the field. The captain's credibility was questioned, and the tour for him was nothing short of disastrous. The tour crashed on the shores of 'more cash'. Reports said that it was quintessentially a case of pilot error; Lara was in the hot seat. Rousseau's press release set out the revised terms of the tour, but it reflected cynicism of a team that clearly did not appreciate the words that graced the release. Both parties, CWI and the WIPA, the release said:

> are satisfied with their agreement, which was reached in a spirit of compromise against a background of international concern. Both parties recognized the historical and social significance of the South African tour and appreciated the high expectations of everyone in the Caribbean South Africa and around the world. The WICB and WIPA would like to acknowledge the constructive support from President Mandela and the Caribbean governments towards achieving an amicable and mutually satisfactory resolution to this dispute.[3]

The 'misunderstanding', as it was described by Rousseau, was damaging in the context of Windies cricket. The team experienced their greatest ever tour defeat, a double white wash in Test and ODIs, back to back.[4]

Lara, Hooper and Shivnarine Chanderpaul, the heart of the batting, failed miserably. They 'failed to apply themselves after they were exposed to the new ball in almost every innings'.[5] The figures were more fictional than real. In the first Test, Lara scored 11 and 7; Hooper 44 and 34; second Test, Lara 4 and 39; Hooper 15 and 8; Third Test, Lara 51 and 79; Hooper 10 and 2; Fourth Test, Lara 4 and 33; Hooper 86 and 20; and the fifth Test, Lara 68 and 14, and Hooper 8 and 10. The ODIs were equally disastrous.

Windies received a whopping 11-0 'white wash'. In summary, noted Martin William, 'on the field West Indies were shamble... Certainly, there was a divided air about the party for much of the tour'. Lara admitted after the fifth Test that 'We are not together as a team'. That appeared an understatement,' and, for the lack of unity, 'Lara had to bear much responsibility.'[6]

The team remained 'soulless', for the entire tour. It could not perform because it had rejected the very principles on which its moral authority and political force rest. It was, in fact, the worst cricket Windies had ever played. There was no ship on which the team could sail because it had poisoned the water that carried it for decades to the land of global respect and dominance.

T:4 White Wash/Black Wash in Test Cricket, 1920–2000

Australia 5	England 0	in Australia	1920–21
Australia 5	South Africa 0	in Australia	1931–32
England 5	India 0	in England	1959
West Indies 5	India 0	in West Indies	1961–62
West Indies 5	England 0	in England	1984
West Indies 5	England 0	in West Indies	1985/86
South Africa 5	West Indies 0	in South Africa	1998/99

The ideological imagery of the team resembled more a party of pirates than a regiment of freedom fighters. The 11-0 defeat could not be brushed under the cricket carpet. There was no room that could contain the debris.

At the end of the tour Lara's captaincy was ended. The crisis revealed his inadequate political clarity. His inability to rise to the emotion of the moment, and the lack of solidarity his team showed within the crisis, confirmed that the outfit was without the critical consciousness that typified the heroic teams of earlier times. The connection and ideological continuity between Lawrence Rowe's rebels of the 1980s, and Lara's men were too much to bear for persons who had opposed the racist regime. Lara's refusal to take on board Caribbean sensibility, despite his problems with Rousseau's leadership, indicated an inadequate comprehension of the circumstances.

The miseducation of Windies cricketers was the basis of the catastrophe. They clearly did not understand the gravity of the history, and it is doubtful if the Board had prepared them for the special encounter with the Mandela Revolution. For the team, it was just another tour despite the rhetoric to the contrary. Lara and Hooper said all the right things about loyalty to Windies. Windies did not only perform at the worst level in their history but they did so at the most critical moment when their pride was expected to be on parade. It was a deeply disturbing moment in a political movement that was alive with democratic possibilities.

No Windies Test team should have been so ill prepared for such a global encounter. To have handled that exchange within the context of business as usual confirmed the belief that nothing sacred was on show. Lara should have entered Johannesburg as the Prince he was dubbed to be in the streets of Port of Spain, and certainly President Forbes Burnham did turn in his grave at the conduct of Hooper's defiance in the face of President Mandela. Guyana, more than any other Caribbean nation, had invested heavily in the effort to bring down apartheid, and its national contribution should have been reflected in Hooper's historic entry.

Furthermore, the crisis revealed, for the first time, the extent to which the generation that entered the team since the exit of Holding and Richards, was disconnected from the politics of the anti-colonial struggle for global dignity. The new era is not rooted in the Caribbean community struggle and campaigns for justice and development. The South African tour was its first significant test in the classroom of global politics and history, and each student in the team failed miserably. But the failure was not simply that of the students. It was also the failure of the teachers that had responsibility for the learning process. The tour was a Caribbean failure.

9

LARA: PRINCE WHO SHOULD HAVE BEEN KING

Brian Lara's brilliance with the bat but less than stellar results as captain of Windies Test cricket was a significant single factor in the first decade of decline. His leadership was the lost treasure of the 'islands'. Potentially a great leader, his reputation at the helm was terribly tarnished in the turbulence of the 1990s decline.

Without paternal protection, the prodigy was targeted, dismantled and discarded. The difference between the trajectories of Sachin Tendulkar and Lara is that India protected and Windies punished. At the first sign of his display of vulnerability and immaturity, Windies threw him to the curb rather than embrace him as an off target missile to be corrected. The East Indies and West Indies each produced a genius. Tendulkar was held up and deified; Lara fell and was flattened. Nationhood nurtured the former; divisive regionalism tortured the latter.

There are no angels in the cricket arena, and Lara was no saint, but more could have been done to save him for Windies, and from himself, during the declining decades. The capacity of West Indian society to diminish the legacies of its great achievers is an endemic retention of colonial culture. Lara was a victim of this lingering colonial practice. When results are great, society is generous; when performance is poor, it is punishing.

To describe the rise and demise of Lara's leadership in the age of performance decline is to detail a tragic chapter in Caribbean history. The cloned child of Garfield Sobers and Viv Richards, mentored by Gordon Greenidge and Desmond Haynes, was raised with but one objective – to lead Windies with bat and brains. No other Test nation on earth was so fortunate to find in an era of doubt, an asset to be leveraged to lead a recovery. A Caribbean gift from God, his bat knew only the boundaries it defined and found. In the doldrums of Windies despair, the team was envied by foes for possessing such an endowment.

Lara came raw and rough, but ready. He was to be honed and polished within and beyond the boundary. In his heroic effort, he was at once magnificent, mysterious and maddening. He was brilliant, boyish and brash. He was fantastic, fanatical and phenomenal. But he was the Windies winner. There was nothing like him. He needed around him a bit longer, a learned leader. This wasn't to be. He could have done more to halt the decline and restore the pride, but his genius with the bat did not translate into brilliance when he took the leadership baton.

At the onset of Windies collapse, Lara emerged as its latest hero, an icon of the global game. A highly artistic and courageous player, he was rated the best batsman in the world on the basis of his spectacular and extraordinary accomplishments, all of which were achieved at a relatively young age.

On April 18, 1994, at the age of 25, he broke the World Test record of 365 runs set by the incomparable Gary Sobers in 1958, when he scored 375 runs against England at Antigua. On June 3, while playing as an 'overseas' professional for Warwickshire County in the English domestic competition, he became the first player to score seven centuries in eight first-class innings. He did not stop there. He proceeded three days later to record the highest first class score, still playing for Warwickshire, against Durham; a massive 501 runs not out breaking the previous best of 424 runs made by Archie MacLaren of Lancashire County 99 years earlier in 1895.

These phenomenal performances were preceded by a majestic innings of 277 Test runs against Australia at Sydney in 1993. The locals, longing for this rare quality in batsmanship, dubbed him the 'Prince of Cricket'. This performance was described by many as the greatest ever played on Australian soil, a fittingly wonderful prelude to the smashing of three world records the following season.

West Indians too, embraced their prodigy with regal language but preferred the designation 'Crown Prince' – recognizing that Gary Sobers would remain the 'King'. With these extraordinary feats, Lara became the latest political icon in the region and his achievements were celebrated in 1994 with the award of the highest national honour of his native Trinidad and Tobago, the Trinity Cross. Finally, to crown it all, he was appointed captain of the Windies Test team in 1996, an announcement that was greeted by a whirlwind of public controversy.

The end of this golden stretch in Lara's career signalled the beginning of rougher patches that further highlighted the systematic decline of Windies. The team over which he towered was easily dwarfed by Richards's prior 'dream team' in which he had made his Test debut. Critics and supporters alike have drawn the inescapable conclusion that his rise to stardom did not impact positively the fortunes of Windies. But this is not how a Windies hero is framed within nationalist ideology. His genius is expected to ignite the team, excite spectatorship and to incite the youth to rise.

The simultaneous fall in Windies performance and the rise of Lara, both against a backdrop of the collapse of West Indian economies and the decay of civil society movements, have contributed to a situation within which postcolonial tensions serve to deeply divide public opinion. No cricket icon has ever had such a divisive impact upon the public imagination in respect of development thinking. The failure of the team to compensate for socio-economic decline led to interpretations of Lara's success as entirely individualistic.

West Indian citizens are not prepared to renegotiate cricket's role within the turbulent but ongoing nation-building exercise. Lara, moreover, was believed to be the leader of this unwelcomed demand for rethinking. The general fear has been that at the end of the discussion, cricket would be unhinged from nationalist sentiments, alienated from community ownership, and thrown headlong into globalized market-driven sports commodification.

Lara, in his own way, was aware that the conceptual integration of the nationalist project and social constructions of the cricket hero, as well as the assumption of their joint mission, are riddled with paradoxes. The vast majority of cricket heroes who preceded him, some of them his role models and career guides, were never financially compensated at a level commensurate with the degree of hero-worship they attracted. Financially distressed and embarrassed stars were casually cast aside as new ones emerged, and Lara encountered a trail of bitterness along the path of his achievement of wealth and fame.

Also, cricket heroes as social icons were expected to subordinate their social and political opinions and actions to the State that offered in return pitiful levels of financial support. Relationships between 'hero' and state were often sour, unhealthy and not mutually supportive. This history and images of dejected has-beens have shaped the social field within which Lara came to define his identity and leadership.

Lara has admitted, on more than one occasion, with a greater telling force after the dismal performance against South Africa in 1998, that a major part of his difficulty in leading the Test team was that players were drawn from different societies in a diverse region where the people are segregated in independent nation-states. But the team in which he made his debut, and those he hero-worshipped as a youth, were also constituted in this way. Something new, therefore, may have surfaced under his regime.

Developments outside of the cricket world are supportive of Lara's suspicion, and the tenor of his explanation. Other public institutions in the region are reeling under the impact of such intra community tension and conflict. The 'spirit' of integrative West Indianness that found solitary and refuge within the bowels of the nationalist cricket culture, and remained marooned there for three decades, is broken and is on the retreat. Today, to proclaim one's West Indian identity in some public places is to invite indiscreet humorous responses. Furthermore, it is now commonplace for West Indians to assert boldly that outside of cricket they are not 'West Indian', and that their interest in the regional integration movement goes no further.

Writing in the Barbados's *Daily Nation* during a heated public ventilation over one of Lara's many controversial actions, Angus Wilkie argued that the 'lack of national unity' is the 'cause of present fragmentation' in West Indies cricket. Despite the lack of political unity and functional nationalism in the 1960s and 1970s, he said, West Indians were 'driven by hope and a vision of West Indian political unity within a reasonably short time. But the reality today is one of doubt and pessimism. Unconsciously, I believe, the gloom has affected our cricket performance.' Wilkie's argument is a compelling one that connects Lara's stated opinion to the wider reality of political governance within the region. For him, West Indies cricket under Lara's leadership was asked to do the impossible – perform at a level of excellence in a 'political void without any unifying force'.[1]

Within a short time, a regional call was for Lara's scalp as captain. His detractors were clear in the view that he was not an effective leader because he did not understand or respect the traditional cultural role of the captain. Critics did not question his ability as a player, but asserted that the magnitude of the office of leader was rather too great for his make of mentality. Senior and junior teammates deeply admired him as a player but were divided in their respect for him as a captain. What they all feared, however, was that officials would strip him of the captaincy, as they publicly threatened to do, leading to his retirement from the Test game.

Lara's supporters responded by stating that removing him as captain was not likely to promote higher levels of performance from him or the team so long as the deepening crisis of West Indian nationalism continues to divide and disable the region. Only the construction of a real, rather than an imaginary West Indian state, that is, an integrated socio-economic and political system of collective responsibility and duties, they said, could create the conditions for West Indies Test cricket resurgence in the age of globalization. The nationalisms of other major competing countries are said to be undergoing substantial strengthening as a result of their strategic responses to the global challenge. In the West Indies, it is said, societies are weakening on account of the parade of parochialism which is exposing their collective vulnerability to the manipulative strategies of larger, more organized nationalistic competitors.

The uniqueness of Lara's social and political context helped to illuminate the extent to which popular democratic processes have shuffled to a halt, and are considered defeated in some quarters. The leadership of many regional public institutions, including those charged with the administration of cricket, is now dictated by a professionally corporate elite who see the abandonment of significant aspects of political sovereignty and national pride as an unavoidable condition of global integration and success. The subjugation of the nation-state, and cricket administration to the rule of traditional big business interests, has combined to create a devastating moral and spiritual assault upon the democratic movements and expectations of mass society. Today, the kinds of working-class communities that have produced Lara are more likely to be seen by the property-owning elites as places that produce incurable criminals rather than cricketing geniuses.

It follows, then, that the renegotiation of cricket culture within the nationalist discourse in an age of globalization is a part of changing class relations in the wider society. The cricketer, as citizen, is a part of the scramble to participate autonomously in the wealth being generated by the refashioned international economy. The division of public opinion on Lara's suitability to represent West Indian aspiration told us a great deal about the nature of these contests.

Working-class citizens are getting around and going beyond the state and traditional arrangements, in seeking freedom to engage non-traditional and international processes. They are attempting to break free of nationalist constraints. They have problematized and destabilized traditional notions of national identity, patriotic pride and social freedom because they see elites financial beneficiaries from the national prostration to North Atlantic financial agencies.

Lara's image and reputation as a cricket icon suffered immeasurably on account of there being no organized indigenous movement that roots post-nationalist cricket culture within the ongoing popular struggle for social equality and material justice. In fact, such campaigns would be received as politically infeasible by ruling political classes on account of their commitment to implement the structural adjustment programmes of the neo-liberal right that is waving in triumph, the flag of the global dawn.

The relegation to memory of earlier cricket triumphalism, and the communal explosion of born-again religious spiritualism, signalled the entrapment of Lara's generation by these economic forces and social discourses. This circumstance highlighted the retreat of the populist movements to which cricket has been hinged since the 1920s. Cricket cannot carry, and certainly not alone, the cross of these crippled political agendas whose leaders, like Lara, are unable to attract and mobilize significant emotional support. What, in fact, the region is trying to understand and cope with is the growing realization that the political process is in crisis, and that cricket culture is in the middle of a paradigmatic shift.

Considerable political turbulence resulted from the nature of Lara's postures and decision-making. The politics of social disenchantment is, in the final instance, the central cause of the discord that surrounds the inner relations of West Indies cricket. It had less to do with Lara's alleged lack of discipline and commitment, though objectively the moral imperatives of the traditional paradigm of national society had been questioned and rejected. The new paradigm has its own distinctive moral features, even though Lara at times appeared to be seeking a reconciliation in order to rescue and harness aspects

(Author) Opening the bowling for the University of the West Indies (Cave Hill) in 2008

Author with Brian Lara at the 3Ws Oval, UWI, Barbados, 2003

Sir Everton Weekes, standing before the West Indies Test Cricket Wall of Fame, 3Ws Oval, Cave Hill, Barbados: The Sir Frank Worrell memorial (3wickets) in the background.

Michael Holding delivering the Sir Frank Worrell Memorial Lecture, UWI, Cave Hill Campus, Barbados, 1998

Lara and Hooper representing the VCXI against India, Queens Park Oval, Trinidad & Tobago, 1997

Handing the Vice Chancellor Trophy to winning Australia's Vice Captain, Michael Clarke, 2008, at the UWI, Cave Hill, Barbados

Author (centre) with Barbados Prime Minister, the late David Thompson, and two nieces, Johnna (left) and Carri (right) during the Australian vs VCXI match at the University of the West Indies, Barbados, 2008

Author (centre) with former teammates at the University of the West Indies, celebrating his Barbados cricket record established in 1994 – taking the most wickets and scoring the most runs in the season.

Author with Chris Gayle during his induction in the 3Ws West Indies Cricket Wall of Fame, UWI, Barbados, 2006

Author with (L to R) brother John, Mum and Dad at the 3Ws Oval VCXI vs Australia, UWI, Barbados, 2003

Michael Holding (L) and Courtney Walsh (R) surrounded by UWI students, Mona Campus, Jamaica, 1996

Launch of the VCXI cricket match project, 1994 (L to R) Alloy Lequay, President of the Trinidad and Tobago Cricket Association, Professor Compton Bourne, Principal of the St Augustine Campus, Trinidad and Tobago, my mentor, Vice Chancellor of UWI, Sir Alister McIntyre and Professor Baldwin Mootoo, Dean, Faculty of Science and Technology.

of the tradition for the future. This, of course, was possible as the best features of colonial cricket were embraced and retrieved by champions of the nationalist phase.

An important feature of Lara's verbal expressions was the indication that while he wished to be admired and respected, he had no warmth for the traditional perception of the cricket hero as an impoverished national ambassador. Nor was he impressed with the social role model construction which he saw as politically manipulative. To some extent he was reacting to the long line of abandoned former heroes who filled his space with hard luck stories about selection and management victimization. In general, he had no time for the probing press, critical spectators, and did not trust administrators, most of whom he saw as his opponents.

Was Lara cut from the same cloth as the 'greats' who went before? When he walked out on his team in England, in 1995, after a dressing room exchange with Captain Richie Richardson, and other senior players, it was reported that his conduct was 'abominable'. There was no precedent for this development in the prior 60 years of Windies Test cricket. This moment, however, should be placed within the context of a threat to do the same thing on his inaugural 1991 tour to England under Viv Richards, after a tense encounter with manager Lance Gibbs, also a Windies legend. Lara discussed both incidents in his book, and casts Richardson and Gibbs in less than positive light.

Lara pulled out of the winter tour to Australia as a result of the fine imposed for his actions in England during the summer, and threatened legal action against the President and the Board. West Indian public was dismayed, but not to the same extent as it was when he withdrew from the training camp called to prepare the team for the Pakistan tour in February 2000 on account of his carnival engagements. In his own words, the responsibility of being the latest icon of West Indies cricket culture became 'too much of a burden' and cricket had 'ruined' his life. At the same time, however, according to Tony Cozier, Lara's refusal to tour Australia was a 'political statement that he wished to see the leadership of the West Indies Cricket Board changed'. In this he succeeded; the debates which followed the debacle resulted in the toppling of Peter Short's presidency.[2]

The events surrounding these aspects of Lara's conduct clearly showed that the West Indian public was deeply divided on his status and leadership. The press reported that mutual dissatisfaction had developed in the relationship between Lara and Captain Richardson, and indicated that it played a significant part in the team's defeat by the Aussies.

The tour to England began in the summer under a dark cloud of despair and internal bickering. Lara did little to set aside public reports that he was critical of Richardson's leadership. Nor did he deny convincingly, reports that he had expressed a desire to lead. Those who backed the claim argued that Lara was tactically superior and had demonstrated this during his service as captain of the Trinidad and Tobago national side and the West Indies youth team. At the mid-point of the tour, open verbal conflict between Lara and his captain threatened its continuation.

The moment of reckoning was a team meeting at which Manager Hall asked players to freely ventilate their opinions. It is reported that Lara made criticisms of the captain's method and style which constituted a call for his stepping down from the leadership. Richardson, it is stated in the Manager's Report, took Lara's assertions personally and responded that he was not going to resign the leadership on account of the egomania and selfishness of any one player, but would readily do so if the team felt that it was in its collective interest. The team stood behind the captain. Lara, it was alleged, feeling betrayed, stormed out of the meeting and stated that he no longer wished to play with the team and announced his resignation from international cricket.

Lara's disappearance from the tour party adversely affected team morale. Manager Hall did all he could to secure his return. The international press had detected that a major crisis was in the touring camp but could not get the details. Lara finally returned to the team and met with President Short, who he said, had agreed to reinstate him without penalty.

Back on board, Lara proceeded to give a series of superlative performances. He scored three centuries in consecutive matches, brought the team back from the brink of defeat, and secured an honourable 2-2 tie in the Test series. The English were confident they could win. Their manager, Ray Illingworth, a former England captain, stated that Lara was all that stood between his team and success. Lara won the man of the series prize and returned home to both cheers and condemnation.

Short's leadership also collapsed on account of the way in which he handled the impasse in England. He was accused by his directors of pandering to Lara's agenda, and condoning his flagrant misconduct. The board did not accept that Short was in a position to make a deal with Lara, and the disciplinary committee proceeded to impose penalties. Lara claimed that he had made a deal with Short by which he was assured that the matter was over and put to rest.

While the selectors were meeting a few weeks later to identify the West Indies team to tour Australia, Lara announced his unavailability citing the need for rest and relaxation. The public was shocked. The Australians were the principal opposition and Lara was the leading batsman. Predictably, the team was well beaten and Lara was vilified in sections of the home media for his lack of commitment to Windies cause. Within a year, however, he was re-appointed captain. But within three years, his regime had collapsed under the weight of 5-0 and 2-0 'whitewashes' at the hands of South Africa and New Zealand respectively. The dominant view in the society was that he reaped as captain, some of what he sowed under Richie's regime.

The amazement expressed by Test legends at Lara's temporary withdrawal from the touring party in England, and subsequent refusal to tour Australia for the World Series Cup, confirms the view that something altogether unfamiliar and non-traditional had surfaced in West Indies cricket. Clarvis Joseph, at the time president of the Leeward Islands Cricket Board, and later vice-president of CWI, described Lara's conduct as the 'height of indiscipline'. Viv Richards expressed the view that these developments would undoubtedly affect the team's future performance. He told the English press: 'I carry no weight with the Board, but I am so dismayed by the affair that, here and now, I volunteer to mediate in an attempt to get a batsman [Lara] better than I ever was, back on track.'[3]

Bob Woolmer, Lara's coach at Warwickshire County, described him as a person who places neither team nor nation before self. Ian Botham, former English superstar, said that Lara 'needs his bum kicked and quickly'. Reflecting on his own career, Botham noted, 'I was no angel but I never let England down.' Colin Croft, former West Indies star, was perhaps most incensed. 'If I had anything to do with the Board meeting,' he said, '[Lara] would not play for the West Indies for a long time.' Michael Holding, Croft's contemporary, added that Lara needed mental help.[4]

The details of Lara's choices and actions that warranted these reprimands became the basis of calls to the WICB to remove him from the leadership of the team. They also served as the reason for reducing his standing as the 'greatest' in the world whose performances for Windies, in difficult and testing situations, were among the most respected in the history of the game. But critically, they were consistent with the call for corporate punishment in schools on the grounds that the brightest children tend to be class disturbers. The facts are not always that clear, wrapped up in superficial opinions as they tend to be. Behind the behaviour can be many messages, including a call for help, conversation, support and, in most cases, just basic understanding.

Lara took on too much, and was asked to carry a weight not seen since George 'Mas' Headley who was dubbed 'Atlas'. He was expected to be the greatest batsman in the world, the best slipper in the team, the best strategic captain, the best off-field spokesman, the best negotiator with selectors and managers, and critically the best collegial leader. His leadership with the bat to win matches and prevent defeats could not be better executed. To halt the decline, even to end it, required a better team and by 2000 his boys played like a posse of indifferent passengers. Despite his heroics, the team fell away. It was commonplace for some pundits to say that his super performances demotivated rather than stimulated his team mates. Only Chanderpaul seemed to rise around him. Others not only looked inadequate but performed that way.

Lara's critics were not always fair, though oftentimes understandable. The passion with which they spoke and wrote raised questions about their capacity as critics to be objective and generous given the terrible state of the Windies environment. Lara wanted to lead and to do well for his team and country, but on new terms and conditions. Tim Hector, critic and commentator, expressed views on Lara's desire to lead that speak to the circumstances that confront West Indian cricket and society in the age of globalization. 'For too long,' he said, 'the West Indies have been playing the aristocratic game. We are resentful of anybody who shows an anxiety to lead and does so openly. We prefer them to behave like British aristocrats, concealing the desire to lead.' Focusing on Lara's bid for the captaincy, he noted that 'we have picked up a disproportionate hostility to Lara because of this. It is precisely that desire and hunger to lead which the West Indies need now to lift it out of the doldrums.'[5]

Richardson was clearly the last heroic captain of the age when national pride more than anything else seemed the motivation for performance on the field. Lara is the first hero of a new paradigm that is characterized by individual performance, privatization through sponsorship, and event and action commodification by global television that has become the principal money earner for the game. There was no turning back. Lara, the first Windies multimillionaire, opened doors for the next generation. His corporate style and global connections became the norm, and articulated his entrepreneurial interests in ways that transcend cricket officials' traditional notions of what is good for Windies cricket.

The comparison of Lara's career trajectory and public celebration with that of Gary Sobers makes the point more clearly. Gary was the genius cricketer who was groomed under the inspirational leadership of Sir Frank Worrell at the end of the 1950s and early 1960s. Indeed, he replaced Sir Frank as captain and super batsman. Sir Gary was celebrated and loved for his heroic performances with bat and ball, and in catching positions that few players imagined they could be effective. His genius was recognized and his performances helped Windies to the top of World Test cricket. Under his leadership, England, Australia and India were defeated between 1966 and 1967, hence the world Test title status.

The series loss against England in 1968 resulted in the public heaping of hatred and vitriol upon Sobers' shoulder. No player in Windies was as vilified, and the calls for his 'neck' were more vicious than anything Lara has experienced. The slaughtering of Sobers for his declaration that gave England an opportunity to win a Test and series, though the manager and team had agreed, went on for the remainder of his career, and for most fans served to tarnish his legacy. Sobers had given Windies cricket more than any other player in history. He gave them a 'world Record', 'World Test Title', and a performance culture that remains unmatched. His art and aesthetic defined as classical, was the icing on a cake. Furthermore, he gave Windies the reputation for having the 'best complete cricketer' the world had ever seen.

None of this prevented the public from lynching the leader for what was a risky decision gone bad. His achievements forgotten, Sobers was denigrated by fans and fellow cricketers who had been diminished by the glow of his genius. The heaping of hysteria upon Lara for his errors as captain and shortcomings as an icon seemed to have overshadowed the great good he did for Windies.

The question of cricket's divorce from nationalism and the abandonment of nationalist sentiment under Lara's influence has more to do with how his generation had been prepared for the challenges ahead. The only rational form of nationalism which they recognize and respond to is one that offers open access to the wider global cash economy. Only seamless entry will hold their imagination in ways that insular nationhood cannot.

The self-confidence that followed Lara's generation, bolstered by a pertinent commercial exposure, and rooted within a postmodern sense of national identity, will slowly provide an important and decisive site for the promotion of a more relevant nationalism. Citizens have shown no intention of delinking identity discourse from cricket culture. It follows, then, that the protection and promotion of the Test game will be an essential part of new strategies of self-empowerment and self-definition.

10

GAYLE: STAR WHO SHOULD HAVE BEEN A HERO

The loss of Chris Gayle, the performance powerhouse of world cricket, to Windies leadership and its sustainability, was a kind of last straw. The giant he became was nurtured in the Jamaican and regional cricket system, from 'little big man' to 'world boss'. Succeeding Lara, he reached his pinnacle during the second decade of the decline. Like Lara, his path to the crease and captaincy was well paved, though riddled with potholes.

Gayle had been out of the Windies Test team at the turn of the twenty-first century when Lara was large and in charge. His invitation by the University of the West Indies (UWI) to play for the Vice Chancellor's XI against Australia in 2003, at the Cave Hill campus, marked his grand return. The 23-year-old scored the maiden century at the campus' newly minted 3Ws Oval, returned that week to the Test fold, rose to the top of the Team, and ultimately clinched the captaincy.

Within five years, he was rated the undisputed global champion of destructive batting. Two triple centuries in Test, and the most feared batsman in the shorter versions of the game, he cemented his status as the 'big man' of Windies, and 'world boss'. As captain, he held an imperial authority over his team, took on an impervious demeanor, and demonstrated an 'own man' mantra that maddened CWI and the heartland of the traditional fan base.

By the second decade, and 15 years into Windies Test decline, Gayle was an effective retreat from Windies cricket. First came his withdrawal of enthusiasm for Test. Then came the controversial surrender of the captaincy, and finally the apparent complete abandonment of interest in Windies cricket. The many 'short and lifting' balls he bowled at CWI rocked its governance structure, leaving it looking weak and wobbley.

The early loss of Gayle to Windies Test was not a singular act. As the senior player of his cohort, he took with him, an entire crop of emerging players. There was undoubtedly a 'Gayle generation' that looked to him as a role model, and was influenced by his actions as an icon. His style and ideas reinforced in them fiercely independent values, already latent and simmering. His considerable charisma led to the institutionalization of an anti-establishment mentality within his entourage.

The execution of Gayle's agenda to assert authority in Windies cricket matters was made possible by the active support of the WIPA, particularly under the leadership of Dinanath Ramnarine. Despite CWI's decision to bestow upon him the captaincy for the series against South Africa, he soon presented it with endless challenges. The final parting of ways was inevitable once, as captain, he had turned up late for duties against England in 2009 allegedly on account of cricketing obligations elsewhere. His team was assembled at Lords, in camp preparing for the first Test encounter. While the coach was taking the team through the drills the captain was missing. His arrival just two days before the match shocked CWI, the officials at the ICC, as well as the English team and officials.

The Test began against the background of public anxiety about Windies readiness and resolve. A missing captain was not a reality ever recorded in the annals of Test. Without prior apology and a spirit of conciliation, Gayle led the team to a resounding defeat with as much time to spare as played. It was as tragic a Test as ever played, with Gayle's personal performance falling below what was expected even in a low-scoring Indian Premier League (IPL) game. Losing a first Test of a tour by 10 wickets inside three days cannot be described in any less than harsh language. As he admitted: 'From when I landed in England it's been rough, and when we lost the game it's been even tougher. We were depressed.'[1]

The Press was not impressed. Apologies were demanded from many sources. The English Captain, Andrew Strauss, expressed his dissatisfaction with Gayle. He spoke in celebration of Test cricket, and made it clear that the game required a minimum level of mutual respect. Strauss stated that his team deserved better, and was not happy wasting their time with Windies.

The outcome of the match was generally anticipated. While Gayle's action did not resemble Lara's rendezvous with his rebel team in London ahead of the South African tour, the demoralized demeanor of his team on the field indicated that the result would be similar. Soulless, and with shame showing on their faces, the team was beaten before it appeared on the field. The captain too looked distracted while his team seemed distraught. A cocktail of confusion and chaos followed the captain out to the middle where he found nothing but misery.

The press gave endless headlines to Gayle's subsequent statement, as captain, that he 'wouldn't be so sad' if Test cricket was replaced by the T20 game. It drew criticisms from former captains, Sir Gary and Sir Viv. He stated that he would not resign the captaincy, as his statement was taken out of context. But long before the 2009 Tour, in his role as captain, there had been signs of his tendency to take the game in this direction. In 2008, during the championship trophy in India, he was fined 30 per cent of his match fee after repeated verbal exchanges with the Australian batsman, Michael Clarke. He was charged with conduct contrary to the spirit of cricket during a Test against New Zealand in March 2006, and was subsequently found not guilty.

In a post-match interview with Anna Kessel, Gayle revealed the nature of his thinking about Windies cricket, and the captaincy especially. 'I didn't want to be captain,' he said, 'I wanted to have more free time…but they actually insisted, so I said okay.' She noted that 'Gayle is reflective in his admission that perhaps he is not cut out for solving West Indies' long standing problems of leadership.

She concluded the analysis where it all began: He is a 'man who lacked personal development', and the 'thought of ridding himself of the burden [of Captaincy] gives him great delight'.[2]

How did Gayle reach this moment? The Lord's Test was not a trial for him as captain. He had bigger fish to fry. His team, filled with youth so respectful of his enormous influence, hardly rose in opposition to the imposition to his actions. In addition, the skipper knew that WIPA was with him down to the wire in confronting CWI and creating a context to make it seem incompetent. There was no weeping in the WIPA. CWI was shamed into being a shadow of its former self.

There were, in addition, influential persons in the West Indies who saw nothing wrong in Gayle's reasoning. 'The man was out there making money, what's the big deal?' This opinion originated in the broadview that it was fair and fine to rip CWI to shreds whenever possible. This perspective by a minority fed into the political posturing of the WIPA's leadership in order to create an ideological environment within which Gayle became the leader of players. With his personal liberties went CWI's credibility. Together, a spiral of player-employer conflict took Windies brand to the cleaners.

In early June 2011, the cricket fraternity gathered in pleasant Queen's Hall, St Ann's, Port of Spain, to attend the WIPA's Eight Annual Players' Award ceremony. As one would have expected, such a gathering of the glittering tribe brought considerable merriment to many men who had worn the maroon with dignity, and a sprinkling of imposters who cared little for the colour they represented. All minds mingled. All hands met and bodies exchanged hugs.

Behind the humanity of the congregation, a tense and tingling sensation was reported as the awards were announced. One reporter told his readers that 'Gayle, who has been shunted out of the team after he accused CWI of leaving him in a lurch during recent injury problems, was named the 2010 WIPA's Cricketer of the Year.' The reporter focused on issues outside of Windies cricket. 'Gayle,' he said, 'who top-scored in the IPL last month with a staggering 608 runs in 12 innings, edged out Shivnarine Chanderpaul, current West Indies Captain Darren Sammy and energetic all-rounder Dwayne Bravo for the top award.'[3]

The emergence of Darren Sammy from the ashes of the burnt Windies was at once a philosophical moment that marked the WICB intent to restore integrity to its business, and a recognition that the time had come to end the confusion over the relationship between captaincy and leadership. The focus on restoring Windies Test cricket leadership in the aftermath of Gayle's assertion that he did not wish to lead, and that the captaincy was thrust upon him, took top priority. His expression of diminished interest in the role was followed by the most powerful posture of all times – that Test cricket is something he could do without! This was the storm that blew through Windies cricket and took the roof off, exposing the crumbling structure and inviting in the elements to subvert the sub-stratum.

Windies Test cricket has a proud and glorious legacy. Some of the greatest men of the region have had the honour of leading the team, most with distinction, some with mixed results, but all were respected beyond the boundary. It was the first occasion that the captaincy was the casualty; a burden unwelcomed in a format of the game most celebrated.

But there is also the question of the legacy of performance excellence. Records were established in Tests that have remained as achievements of Caribbean civilization, long dedicated to making noble contributions to the World. Those records were established by men with considerable commitment to cricket and society. Sir Everton's feat of four consecutive Test Centuries made against India, in India in 1948/49, for example, stands today as a sentinel to Caribbean pride. Sir Gary, Sir Viv, Sir Frank, Sir Clyde, Sir Wes, Sir Richie, Sir Andy and Sir Curtly, all knights of the Caribbean's brightest days, have illuminated the path for a people emerging from long nights of colonial darkness.

To imagine a Windies Captain, then, not fully on board, was to experience swimming in the cold, unclear waters of London's Thames. The British media could hardly contain their rage, knowing well that the thing they respected – Test cricket – had been injured by someone expected to preserve it as a sanctuary.

Sammy was called upon to refloat the ship – to bring it up and allow the Caribbean sun to shine upon its tattered mask. The responsibility was enormous given the depth of despair left behind. Sammy immediately signalled his capacity and competence as a leader of Test cricket, beyond and within the boundary. He was described by many, as an average Test cricketer who ascended to the throne, yet none could say that his heartland was not more than adequate for the mission. He was refreshing in every aspect of his leadership. He was not just a captain on the field; he sought to restore the pride to the enterprise.

The return of spirit to Windies under Sammy's leadership also confirmed the extent of the damage done by Ramnarine within the context of the WIPA's approach to achieving its end. Sammy spoke to the public, and to the youth as a mentor. The UWI honoured him in his community. He knew that within his team the roots of the old dispensation were still alive and spreading. He was equipped with a capacity to read his reality, and expected at some time that the forces he had faced down would again rise up. The WIPA, especially, kept its peace, waiting.

Sammy's tenure was meant to be restorative. He was charged with replacing the roof and giving a view throughout the widest window to young players placed in his charge. His role was no different to that expected of Gayle when CWI invested in his ability to lead. Sammy's entry, then, was surrounded by considerable internal ill will, despite the Board's assurance that he was well guarded and regarded. There were moments, of course, when the price he paid seemed excessive, but his considerable courage as a cricketer, and his regard for the legacy of Windies kept him going – all the way to winning the T20 World Cup – not once, but twice.

The CWI–WIPA clash over the decision to select Gayle dominated Windies cricket environment in 2012. The choice of Sammy as leader and captain served to widen the context of controversy. Comments made by Gayle ignited the ire of CEO of CWI, Ernest Hilaire, who took personal umbrage and responded. The press reported that Gayle had stated it was the intention of Hilaire to bring harm to his career. Hilaire had good reason to believe that his contributions to cricket administration were placed in bad light. Gayle refused to retract or apologize, and remained outside the team for over a year. Sammy, meanwhile, had consolidated his status as an effective leader and captain.[4]

Gayle's responses remained consistent: 'What should Chris Gayle apologize for and what should Chris Gayle retract?' This stance, the *Daily Express* reported, meant that he was 'likely to remain persona non grata and out of the West Indies team'. 'He is not one for retracting words', the paper reported, and his defiance had 'brought him into conflict with authority more than once in the past'. The Caribbean Community (CARICOM) was invited into the heart of the dispute, and once again Windies cricket was placed in the political arena for adjudication. Fortunately, the Prime Ministers of CARICOM adopted a balanced approach to resolving the crisis.[5]

After the disaster in May 2009, Gayle was willing to give up the 'burden' of captaincy. He said this much then. Then came the greatest tragedy of all in a Windies home tour. The Bangladesh team arrived in July to challenge Windies. Within a week of the announcement of the tournament industrial relations aggression surfaced leading to the WIPA pulling the team from the tournament. The abandonment of the series, the first action of its kind in a home series, was not surprising giving the nature of the WIPA's approach to the challenges facing Windies.

Sammy, and a few other players, did not support the strike, and were retained by selectors when a new team was assembled to contest the visitors. Led by Floyd Reifer, with Sammy as Vice-Captain, the Series, both Tests and one day internationals (ODIs) were lost, but most games were closely fought and the ancestral spirit of Windies cricket was rekindled.

Back to back events in 2009 created a crescendo of calls for the ending of Gayle's captaincy. CWI was placed under tremendous pressure to see what the public had been demanding. The team was due to tour Australia in November that year, and the expectation was that a change was required.[6]

Chairman of Selectors, Clyde Butts, said that the composition of the team was fit for the purpose:

> I think we have a good combination and an experienced team which I expect to do very well. We have selected a balanced team…; we have a quality bowling attack, and a very good batting line-up with players who have performed on the international stage. We believe the players all have the ability to deliver at the highest level.[7]

What was missing was leadership. Gayle's results as captain were poor – winning 3 Tests out of 14, and 13 ODIs out of 38. The highlights of this performance, however, are significant. Under his captaincy, Windies did win two series in ODIs, including an away victory against England in 2008, and against the touring Sri Lanka. He also won the first Test against South Africa in Johannesburg, while the series slipped away.

As late as June 2011, the 'Gayle–WICB crisis' had not been resolved, despite high level political interventions. On the 24th, the WICB issued a public statement which was widely reported in the media. It followed a meeting with Gayle and the WIPA's President and Vice-President Dinanath Ramnarine and Wavell Hinds, respectively.

In no other cricketing nation was a player locked into such an intensive combat with his board. The preamble to the statement noted that 'exception efforts had been made' to establish 'a productive working relationship' with the captain, but that his 'pattern of behavior' culminated in conflict and the making of statements 'unbecoming for a professional sportsman' who would be desirous of playing within 'the Windies team environment'.

Gayle's representative disagreed and charged that CWI had '[ill] treated him and had tarnished his name and reputation.' When Gayle sought an explanation for his exclusion from the team, CWI noted that his media comments had 'created much ill-will with team management' and that unless there was a 'settling of differences, it would be difficult to see how the parties could harmoniously function.'

CWI insisted that Gayle had to agree to 'respect rules and regulations' and be willing to 'engage in a constructive manner on matters which are of concern to him'. Also, that he needed to respect selection criteria and that CWI would write to him on such matters. According to the statement, the WIPA's leader Ramnarine, opined that the 'WICB has no business writing to players, and under no circumstances should WICB be writing to Gayle, or any player for that matter, as it is his view that the players are not in the employ of WICB'.[8]

Gayle remained in a 'wait and see' mode in respect of Windies cricket. He offered himself for tournaments selection that suited his agenda and concerns. His willingness to play in major championships, such as T20 and ODI World Cups, brought mixed comfort to Windies selectors, given his negative attitudes to Test cricket. His commentary on Windies cricket remained generally critical of officials, including legends who are tasked with formatting recovering strategies and fostering discipline within the team.

Following CWI decisions to non-select senior players who were engaged in the leadership of the tour 'walk out' in India in 2014, Gayle took to the media to express his opinion. Chairman Lloyd went to considerable lengths to explain selection policy and team objectives in respect of planning for the World Cup, describing the event as a spring board for a rebuilding exercise.

The exclusion of Dwayne Bravo and Kieron Pollard, especially, from the squad enticed Gayle to describe the decision as 'victimization' and 'ridiculous'. CWI , once again, took offence and noted that 'the rant against selectors' was a breach of the code of conduct. The disciplinary charge against Gayle, however, was dropped on a technicality. Charges must be brought against an offender within ten days of the alleged commission of the offence, and CWI was not in compliance.⁹

Gayle is without doubt the 'world boss' of T20 cricket. The cricket community in the past five years has seen his extraordinary capacity. He is the 'king' of the IPL, the Big Bash, and the English circuit, and threatens daily to set records that seem out of reach for the best elite cricketers. His global image as the entertainment icon has defined his reputation as the 'freelance filibuster', the 'big six hitter', and the 'Mr Cool' of the festival circuit. He is the face of globetrotting 'money cricket', the 'big bang and buck' champion of the crowd that cares little about 'Test cricket' and other such traditional constructs.

In 2015, in order to complete the caption, Gayle took advantage of lowly Zimbabwe in a qualifier in Canberra. He struck the first double century in any World Cup – 215 runs off 147 balls. Balls flew to all curves of the boundary, and a massive 16 sixes also equalled the previous record held by two big hitters – Rohit Sharma of India and A.B. de Villiers of South Africa. He showed no mercy on the minnows. Maybe it had something to do with his keenness to establish that when it matters – the World stage – he is the top performer.

The performance followed a long dry spell in the short game he loves, and there was talk of his retirement as big runs had dried up. Zimbabwe, rather than South Africa, paid the price for his restored passion. In some way his six hitting was a precursor to what was coming next at the Gabba when he established another record, the first cricketer to hit 600 sixes in the T20 game. Playing for the Melbourne Renegades in the Big Bash League against Brisbane Heat, he struck two sixes to establish the record. In the innings, he also racked up a tally of 653 fours, just a dozen short of the 'fours' record.

While CWI seemed to have come to the end of the line with Gayle in terms of the role he could play in rebuilding the pride of Windies Test cricket, the World continues to benefit from his theatrics. No other cricketing nation faces this condition. His freelance, global, 'get them' approach, has handsomely enriched cricket investors.

At the end of 2015, as Windies officials looked to the future without Gayle's presence, David Saker, coach of Melbourne Renegades, boasted that he could 'get the best out of Gayle'. He averaged less than 20 when he played for the Sydney Thunder in the 'Big Bash', but he found a home with Renegades, Saker said, and 'we are excited about working with him'. Reporting that Tom Moody, the Renegades manager, has a 'good relationship with Chris', Saker added that 'We have got a good idea of how to handle him and how to manage him.'

What then does Gayle respond to within the Renegades setup that he cannot find within Windies? How is it that they know how to 'manage him' and his Windies cannot get a handle on it? The answer seems to begin with Saker's expectation of him. For them he is just a runs machine, pure and simple. There is no more to it. He is not a 'role model', a community icon, nor an inspirational leader for the youth. Simply put, said Saker, 'he'll win us games of cricket and that's what we expect him to do.' Here, then, is where the Windies developmental model runs into conflict with the 'Big Bash' mentality. This is where Gayle seemed to have found his niche.[10]

Meanwhile, Windies fans, and lovers of Test, continue to wish for him to wear the maroon. In Australia, the backlash came against his Big Bash cash in, with cricket fans referring to him as the 'Gayle Farce', and urging him to 'go home' and play for his country. This is understandable; no Australia cricketer could turn his back upon his country's Test obligations and survive as selectable. This view is not lost on the Aussies who know how to manage him while seeking to keep Windies cricket on its knees.

The global gain of Gayle has, therefore, not always been a Windies benefit. The matter is choice, and the issue of expectation is all a part of this discursive predicament and maybe the balance will be found post-Gayle. He speaks of his return to Windies, to Tests, but to build a Test team is not a simple matter of collecting who is suddenly available. The English established a model with the Pieterson non-selection – the country's finest batsman but also the most problematic.

Fans and fraternity are not prepared to renegotiate for Test cricket a new, diminished role along the rocky road that nation-building inexorably has to travel. Like Brian Lara at the end of the twentieth century, Gayle is the titular twenty-first-century leader of the redefining process. The general fear at the level of regional political leadership, and amongst the grassroots, is that cricket will unhinge itself completely from nationalist sentiments, and free fall into the monetary embrace of foreign-controlled, globalized market forces. While Caribbean citizens are generally satisfied with the idea of having millionaire cricketers in their communities, the cost of losing Test cricket respect seems unbearably high.

11

RAMDIN RAMS RICHARDS: BRAVO BERATES WINDIES

Two events along the decline trajectory stand out more than others, as prime indicators of the sold soul of Windies cricket. In both instances the world was invited to witness the expressions of the internal decay that signalled the decline of principles, purpose and philosophy. In both instances players with average records of attainment, both in terms of Windies legacy and contemporary expectations, weakened the monument built by prior generations.

A.   Ramdin Blasts the Master Blaster

The demeaning act took place during Windies Tour to England in 2012. It was the third and final Test at Edgbaston, a home of Windies legacy performance over decades of dominance. As was the recent norm, Windies were tragically underperforming. The Test series was already lost, England having won the first Test at Lords by 5 wickets, and the second by 9 wickets at Trent Bridge.

Denesh Ramdin had been recalled to the team as wicket keeper after two years, replacing the inexperienced Carlton Baugh. Against the South Africans who toured the West Indies in 2010, he scored just 63 runs in 3 Tests and 34 runs from 5 ODIs. The tour to England, until the third Test, seemed like a repeat performance of poverty at the crease. He appeared 'at sea' to the swinging ball, and with poor footwork was easy pickings for England seamers and spinners.

Ramdin was a senior player in the team, though this was not reflected in his scores. At age 27, he had achieved an unacceptable Test average of 22.28 from 44 games. There was only one century in his column, suggesting a scoring calamity if not catastrophe. His record suggested a race to the bottom rather than a rise to occasions.

His maiden century was an innings against the English in a drawn Test at Barbados in which runs flowed like rum on a golden sand beach. England in the first innings scored 600 for 6 declared with Andrew Strauss scoring 142, Ravi Bopara, 104, Alastair Cook, 94, and Paul Collingwood, 96. Ramdin's 166 was in a Team total of 749 declared, an innings in which Ramnaresh Sarwan made 291, with 50s from Devon Smith, Shivnarine Chanderpaul and tail ender Jerome Taylor.

Cook returned in England's second innings to score 139. Ramdin's century did not precipitate prosperity. Since then he played in 18 of Windies 29 Tests. Recalled for the English tour he managed in the first two Tests to muster a meagre 51 runs 4 innings – 1, 43, 1, and 6. In addition, his glove work was less than golden, inviting frequent negative comments on his inconsistency.

It was a tournament in which Windies showed further signs of deteriorating beneath the dismal, and the media could manage to make no favourable comments in the face of a mountain of mediocrity. Sir Viv was a part of the media, offering expert insights into games as well as commentary on the growing expectation of Windies failure. Ramdin's poor performance stood out like a beacon above a rocky beach. Sir Viv addressed his circumstance by stating that 'for some reason, he has deteriorated in such a big way. Just the way he is walking back, he looks like a totally lost guy.' He referred to the 'immature' attitude of the team and suggested that 'these individuals need to think about the requirements to play at this level.'[1]

On reaching a century on the fourth day of the Test, and with Tino Best batting at no. 11 scoring a massive 95 and stealing the partnership show, Ramdin responded to Sir Viv. He had clearly planned the theatrical moment. He removed his helmet, reached into his trousers pocket, pulled out a white sheet of paper, and raised it aloft with both hands before the crowd and cameras. The words, written in bold capitals, said 'YEA, VIV, TALK NAH.'

The unfortunate nature of the intervention, in addition to its intent to disrespect the legend, shocked the cricket world as media headlines howled the story across the globe. It was unimaginable that this kind of action could take place at the crease of a Test. It was a protest that spoke to the very immaturity Sir Viv had indicated was a concern in Windies camp.

Never before had a Test cricketer used the crease to score media points against a fellow cricketer. It smacked of a surreal circumstance in which a teenager had shouted in the neighbourhood that he was grounded by his father for not doing his school work, said an outraged blogger. Critically, it was a wounding choice of words that sought to diminish the most globally celebrated and feared Windies cricketer in its age of dominance. With an average of 50 from 121 Test, Sir Viv had a right to offer a fair comment on Ramdin's under par average. In Trinidadian vernacular, he blasted Sir Viv before the world. The jester had abused the king, but there was no humour in the hubris. It was raw, vicious, and vindictive. Only an imploded mind could have performed this act of contempt and self-abasement.

It was, however, just another indicator of what C.L.R. James had called the 'welfare of state of mind'. Every West Indian understood what Ramdin had told Sir Viv. Every Windies legend felt that in some way West Indies dignity was betrayed that day at Edgbaston. It is a place where Lance Gibbs, Rohan Kanhai, Alvin Kallicharan, Brian Lara, Derek Murray, Rudi Webster and others had laid a foundation dedicated to Windies presence and excellence. Ramdin outraged, served as a canopy over the credentials of these Windies heroes.

Public reactions were swift as they were sensible. There was a call to heal the wound. Michael Holding, who has used his media profession as a pulpit of principles and passionate expression of concern for the corroded dignity of Windies cricket, immediately felt the disdain Ramdin had dumped on the respected elder of the tribe. Nothing less than an apology and a fine by Windies management could suffice under the circumstance, he argued. It was a breach, not only in the Windies fraternity, but of the ethical code of the game that had never before witnessed such a broad side.

The meltdown of Ramdin's mind was not phenomenal in the least. To frame his fracas in terms of an interpersonal exchange is to misread what was communicated, and why. Ramdin's message was as coded with culture markers as can be imagined. The words themselves might appear empty in their simplicity, but the loaded cargo of the construction speaks to the state of mind that has taken root in Windies cricket culture in the era of erasure and the rejection of erudition. It represents also the rise of the 'fast food' state of mind that struggles to know right from wrong.

Ramdin's awareness of the unacceptable nature of the theatrics did not prevent his publication. It was an event planned with the intention to excavate his actions from critical review. The shallowness of his strategy served to communicate something much more mundane than it was profane. It was simply that a team was surrounded by the ruins of performance, was lacking in historical sense and social sensibility, and corrupted by a culture in which care and caution, reason and respect, were placed on the back burners. The refusal to reflect upon the truth of his failure or value the worth of Sir Viv's criticism produced instead in Ramdin an impulse to impale an elder.

Sir Viv who stands at the pinnacle of the Windies Test pyramid, constructed by three generations of craftsmen was targeted by an insolent incumbent bent on rejecting critical observations intended to help rather than hinder. Ramdin's choice was not unexpected; neither should it be accepted as incidental. He was the spokesman for a posse that posed the greatest single threat to the legacy of appropriate conduct that had been the norm. This too, had a purpose and a cause. It was this. The only way to remove the shadow that reveals the absence of light is to flatten the edifice that is the cause. Herein resides the thinking, or lack thereof, that produced the offending paper.

The losing team at Edgbaston stood in stark comparison with that led by of Sir Viv's which had never lost a Test series to England. Ramdin sought a solution to his predicament by obliterating the voice he wished not to hear. Sir Viv was the symbol of the history in which Ramdin felt trapped, producing media messages that highlighted his inability to rise, shine and score. In an expected moment Ramdin took his eyes off the ball that was England's bowlers and took a swing instead at the sage on his own side.

Silenced in the Test series, but vocal before society, Ramdin's revelation emerged as further compelling evidence of the erosion of the knowledge base of Windies players. That he had scored only his second century in as many years at the crease, and in a series already badly lost, should have sponsored a more in tuned sensibility. Instead, oblivious to the environment of the tournament, the mini-moment of his triumph exploded internally as an achievement of liberation and salvation. The inability to gauge the diminished dimensions of his century as Windies went down in ignominy meant that he was without poise and balance in the middle.

The use of a paper bullet to shoot the 'Master Blaster' spoke volumes, therefore, as the noise echoed across Birmingham and connected the cricket world from Brisbane to Barbados, Jamaica to Johannesburg. Viv's response was precise, befitting the mind that had mastered the art of proportion. He described Ramdin's century as akin to a goal scored in the last seconds of a game in which one's team was down 5-0. This relationship of time to circumstance did not register with Ramdin simply because he did not appreciate the interconnection between self, team and society. At that moment, his mind bore no professional relations to his team or to the society that he represented.

In this regard, Ramdin's intention was to legitimize the disconnection of being a cricketer from the West Indies with what it has been to be a Windies cricketer. The gulf he sought to construct being himself and Sir Viv, the legends and the losers, was the source of his peace of mind. By burning the bridge over which he had travelled to Edgbaston meant that there was no need to look back to Richards and the other bridge builders. He had crossed over into a promised land of plenty without performance, and the voice of Richards was the source of a truth he preferred unspoken.

In the West Indies most fans concurred that there was a bridge burning. They also understood that Sir Viv was waving the warning flag from his bank while Ramdin was raising his with rage on the other. The water under the bridge had been troubled for a long while, and now it was muddied. Ramdin after being mauled by the media offered to buy Sir Viv a drink, but the river remained far too turbulent to navigate.

There was a call for the decentred, descending cricketer to be sent as an intern to the Academy for a 'mind job', but this was not considered an official option. A few in the Establishment called for a penalty but the majority thought Ramdin's action a 'fair comment'. It was a clear indication that cricket officials had lost either consciousness or courage. The case file was quickly closed on the shooting, and sent to the archives where it rested, until retrieved two years later for the next entry; a memo from the WICB by which Ramdin was invited to captain Windies Test.

B. Bravo – Mumbai before Windies

The news of Dwayne Bravo's bouncer crashed into the head of Windies cricket and sent it reeling. Fans and officials went into shock as the global media went into a feeding frenzy, fanatically seeking out comments on the news out of Delhi. Indian fans of Windies ran for cover in order to avoid the call to comment.

The *Hindustan Times* dropped the bomb! It reported part of an alleged transcript of an interview it purported to have had with Bravo in which he proclaimed that his professional and personal commitment to his Indian Premier League (IPL) team, Mumbai Indians, transcended that held for Windies. Persons in India faxed, scanned and emailed, and texted press extracts of the transcript to the Caribbean. There was disbelief and dismay that a Windies senior cricketer could publicly diminish and dismiss his team and 'nation'.

The transcript makes for interesting reading. It contains well-spoken, precise and passionate words. The mind of an intelligent man was clearly at work, subtle in some ways, but blunt and direct in others. When asked about the IPL, his reported response was specific. 'I believe I am a Mumbai Indian at heart,' he said, 'and they think the same way' about me. When asked about the comparisons being made between Brian Lara and Sachin Tendulkar, his reported response skilfully segued: 'I am privileged to have played with both.'[2]

Then came the bouncer! Where is your greater love, Mumbai Indians or Trinidad and Tobago, he was asked. 'Of course Trinidad and Tobago. It's my country. Mumbai Indians come second, Trinidad and Tobago first and the West Indies third.' The story was read as final confirmation by a senior player that Windies cricketers cared little for the legacy, or the future. This was finally understood as the primary reason for the Test team's performance decline. Without deep, passionate commitment, the critics said, Windies Test cricket was doomed. For millions, Bravo's reported declaration represented the new consciousness that appeared casual on the field and carefree in defeat.[3]

Indian society was deeply divided by the reported declaration. Some citizens were pleased that their IPL could garner such lofty loyalty, but others were disturbed by the ideological significance and political implication of the choice. What if, they asked, had an Indian player placed his personal cash choice before national duty? Pundits agreed that Indian society would never accept national subversion from a cricketer. Only in the West Indies, it seemed, could this circumstance enter the realm of the 'new normal'.

There was no surprise in the inner corridors of Windies cricket.

While it was shocking in the outer rim, the inner core had surmised that this ranking was real, and that Bravo's business model was but the tip of the iceberg. The cold truth could not be brushed away. Bravo's honesty was consistent with the relative power of the IPL to purchase and extract players from the grip of CWI that had long lost moral authority over senior players it bred and fed. The reported declaration by Bravo allegedly broke no CWI laws, but simply widened its awareness of the enormity of the problem.

The public, in turn, read the story as another episode in the saga of betrayal and subversion by Windies senior players. Bravo was influential in the IPL for his batting and his ranking was reflected in his banking. He was, according to business experts, as entrepreneurial a cricketer as it is possible to be.

Beyond the mass media the narrative was read as evidence of the final internal crumbling of Caribbean public consciousness. The liberation ideology that contributed to Windies Test supremacy, it was said, was now obsolete, and replete with visionless values. The ease with which Bravo is said to have rolled out his business model suggested that his mind had long been made up.

The predicament, then, for Windies was how to move forward with Test players unlikely to give their all for the team. Commentators for a decade had been speaking about Windies easiness in the field – the cool dudes in shades who saw giving their all as a risk to injury and therefore a loss to the IPL. But Test cricket when played with restraint and fear of injury shows horribly on TV screens. The casual and unprofessional are exposed. They are viewed as a kind of vandalism of values long invested in and respected.

In the case of Bravo, the most exuberant and physically expressive of player, academics and critics read the declaration as more than a detrimental denouncement of Windies cricket. His alleged choice indicated that he was spiritually disconnected from the soul of the Windies. It was not a part of his idealized future. His 'home' was a very specific place, two rather than twenty islands. On his menu, these two islands were the appetizer and the IPL the entrée.

How then did Bravo continue to represent Windies? Two perspectives emerged in an effort to meaningfully answer this question. First, it was suggested that since Windies cricketers no longer felt a sense of passionate commitment to the Test team, their participation was merely a professional act, more aligned to cash requirement than country committment. Second, they were seeking to build Windies cricket as a new finance industry which offered a lavish living outside of national service. Their desire was to politicize cricket, explode its ideology of resistance and nation-building, and put in place a new professional practice that gives primacy to the individual 'pay day' rather than 'national pride play'.

Bravo's ranking, then, was more than an expression of cash before country. It was part of the deconstruction of Windies cricket, taking it away from its roots in the regional race, class and culture agenda and planting new seeds in global commerce where national boundaries are irrelevant, inhibiting and irritating.

Three years later, CWI appointed Bravo captain of the ODI team to lead the series against the visiting Zimbabweans. He replaced the dedicated and disciplined Darren Sammy.

The Grand Slam – Bravo Walks Off

In 2014, Bravo returned to India as captain of Windies ODI team. Within weeks, the captain slammed Windies cricket with its greatest ever public disgrace. He led his team off the tournament and out of the country, bringing shame to the game and the risk of bankruptcy to CWI, and Windies cricket in general. It was, again, an historic moment hatched in large part in the mentality of the man who was reported to have declared his diminished commitment to Windies cricket.

It was on the eve of the fourth ODI in Dharamsala, Friday, October 17, 2014, that Windies players, led by their captain and spokesman, walked off the tour. Bravo spoke of challenges his players were experiencing with their union, WIPA, and indicated that the team if necessary was willing to take things into their own hands. The dispute was not with the WICB, their employer, but with their union.

The WIPA had signed an industrial relations agreement with CWI that would govern playing conditions on tour. Wavell Hinds, its president, was reported to have said that the agreement was 'not perfect' but was a deal that promised stability and agreeability between players and employer.[4]

Bravo is reported as saying that before the tour had begun on October 8, the agreement between the WIPA and CWI was problematic, and that players were of one mind in withdrawing their services from the tour. The players, he is reported as saying, are 'sticking together, despite what's going on'. Sanjay Patel, secretary to the Board of Control for Cricket in India (BCCI), reported that he did his best to persuade Bravo and his team to continue the tour, but there seemed to be 'little thought' given to the future of the game and the relations between Windies and Indian cricket.[5]

Ironically, Bravo whose heart was reported to be in India had now confronted Indian cricket with its greatest embarrassment and financial predicament. He insisted that in his decision and deliberations he had received the support of his team, including T20 Captain Darren Sammy and Test Captain Denesh Ramdin.[6]

Senior batsman, Marlon Samuels, however, declined to be included in Bravo's consensus, and declared that he wanted no part of his leadership. 'The main thing first was West Indies cricket,' he said. 'My focus,' he said, 'was just on playing some cricket. I just needed to finish this tour and then I would have asked questions.' Bravo denied this, and added that 'Samuels was supportive of the decision as he attended some meetings and was a part of the conversations. The team members and I, as captain, were nominated and accepted the responsibility to correspond on behalf of the players,' Captain Bravo said, 'and I will continue to do so as designated.'[7]

CWI, compromised, embarrassed and feeling the pains of possible crippling financial liabilities, issued a statement 'blaming the collapse of the tour – with a fifth one-dayer, a Twenty20 match and three Tests all remaining on the itinerary – on players'. It indicated that the calling off of the Tour did not come from its leadership, and rests entirely with Bravo and his men.[8]

Presenting itself as an innocent party in the crisis, CWI did not take responsibility for the players' conduct, but situated Bravo at the centre of an action whose outcome would be a deep-seated damaging of Windies cricket. It did not anticipate this action by Bravo's men, simply because it seemed farfetched, and unprecedented.

But there was no sound reason to have assumed that Bravo would not have encouraged the disgruntled players to humble themselves and complete the assignment once started. CWI was clearly idealistic, and underestimated the real nature of Bravo's political attitude towards Windies cricket, and officials in particular. It also reported that in his initial communication to the WIPA's president and CEO, Mr Hinds, Bravo chose to use inflammatory language and issue 'a clear threat to cause injury to West Indies Cricket'.[9]

This statement followed an earlier report attributed to Bravo in which he wrote:

> We wish to make it very clear that should the players be forced to take matters into their own hands, we will not hesitate to take the appropriate action as we see fit. We will hold you [Hinds] and the WIPA Board, who support this process [signing the MOU with the WICB] liable.[10]

CWI, then, had reasons to believe that Bravo's declaration was not to be taken lightly. Statements attributed to him, plus earlier discourses about his personal Windies ranking, were enough to have created worry in the minds of officials. Bravo was clearly no man to mess with within Windies cricket, given his power and status as captain. CWI had created an icon with authority and energy capable and willing to incite the passive and the indifferent.

Bravo's bouncer struck home. 'It was a bomb waiting to detonate, wreaking more damage to West Indies cricket, which, after two decades of collapse, can hardly withstand anymore.'[11] Dave Cameron used social media to assert: 'This feels like Terrorism. You destroy a region's heritage over an internal dispute. Unbelievable.' The BCCI claimed damages from CWI for the incompletion of the tour totalling US$41.97M, a sum that was beyond the Board's capacity pay.[12]

CWI, faced with the cancelled tour, a captain's hostility, and massive financial claims to liability, had good reason to feel that 'terrorism' had taken root within Windies cricket. The reign of terror to which the president alluded could only further sink Windies. Bravo was stripped of the captaincy and not selected for the 2015 World Cup. CWI offered him a retainer contract, which according to chairman of selections, Clive Lloyd, 'means he has not been thrown out.'

SECTION THREE

RETURN OF THE
WEST INDIES

12

BACK TO THE FUTURE: EDUCATE, NEGOTIATE, DON'T VIOLATE

While the world, it seemed, had lost its mind celebrating the 500th anniversary of Columbus's violent invasion of the Caribbean, 1992 was also the year in which Windies Test Cricket was approved as a subject for formal discussion in UWI's classrooms.[1]

The academic campaign that followed was considered a necessary prerequisite to consolidate the performance excellence of players. An objective was to critique the consciousness that enhanced the decline and outline the path to restoration.

The programme was conceptualized and created as a teaching and research instrument dedicated to discerning trends and patterns in the development of Windies cricket within its global context. An accredited academic curriculum entitled 'West Indies cricket since 1790' was offered to students who were expected to participate in research-based conversations about the present and future of Windies. In addition, the Sir Frank Worrell Memorial Lecture series was intended to focus public attention upon these trends and patterns.

Sir Frank had been the umbilical link between Windies cricket and the UWI. He had served as a Director of Student Services at the Mona and St Augustine campuses, played for the Mona campus in the Jamaica Senior Cup competition, and was buried at the Cave Hill campus in Barbados. His pedagogy called for an intimate bond between academia and cricket and he was known for insisting that cricketers acquire a university education whenever circumstances allowed.

My task as Director of the Cricket Research Centre was to bring these strands together and establish a template for the University to serve the broad stakeholder interests of Windies cricket. It was important to theorize the extent to which Test performance was sustainable at the level of excellence. It was also critical that the UWI should participate in the process of ensuring that the excellence achieved was not completely lost. Cricket studies became a normal part of the University's overall academic mandate, and the CCR was its first institutional response.[2]

The primary objective of the University was to establish a cricket research and teaching institute that would serve as a supportive hub for Windies cricketers, past, present and future. The transfer of knowledge from one generation to another is considered a vital aspect of sustaining excellence. This formal context was lacking, and Windies cricketers were denied formal access to relevant knowledge.

The second phase in this project was to provide a new cadre of Windies cricketers better suited to the age of globalization that was already beginning to redefine the game. It was determined within the classroom that West Indies would be hardest hit by these global forces. Test cricket was deemed particularly vulnerable and the UWI was in a good position to blow the whistle and round up the troops for a war of self-defence.

Noah had his sceptics. That is the way it always is. The UWI was surrounded by multiple oppositions, some of which were hostile to its intervention. Resources were found to transform the basic cricket field at the campus into an international venue that would carry the name 'The 3Ws Oval'. This was done in short time, and the University was positioned to host the visiting Australia team in 2003, and ODI World Cup warm-up matches in 2007. International broadcast quality floodlights were installed in 2006 and stood in contrast as a sign of the future when in 2007 Kensington Oval, just a mile away, was flooded with darkness and the region shamed as the closing minutes of the World Cup final were played under moonlight.

Additional infrastructure preparations were completed in the years after 1995. The first indoor cricket school in the Caribbean was built; it provided for six netted practice lanes and floodlighting. The Sir Gary Sobers Indoor School, as it was called, has remained the faculties' leader on the island. From the classroom, then, cricket studies were relocated to the fine clinical training facilities, and the Cave Hill campus was established as the premier coaching and training hub for Windies Test cricketers.

The UWI, took critical responsibility for the upgrade of Windies Test cricket. It also developed a strategy to produce student cricketers for the national and international levels. The first effort was to persuade the Barbados Cricket Association (BCA) that a student team should be allowed to compete at the national elite level. This was a major campaign. With the compliance of Tony Marshall, President of the BCA, the Campus team was granted special entry. This was the most radical development in decades of Barbados cricket. Students were positioned to compete in national competitions, and to demonstrate the effects of the training programme on field performance.

Floyd Reifer, senior Barbados and former Windies player, was brought on board to coach and lead the student team. Within two seasons, the students established national dominance. All national teams were beaten and existing records of achievement broken. The University demonstrated the role it could play in the provision of research, teaching and learning while being the top team in the national premier league. Quality performance requires research facilities and tactical innovation. At the UWI, these elements were put in place and the results were evident.

It was then time to engage CWI with a view to allowing a universities and colleges student team to participate in its regional tournaments. This negotiation proved less challenging. Under Julian Hunte's presidency, a team called the Combined Campuses and Colleges (CCC) was welcomed to participate as an equal of the six national teams – Jamaica, Guyana, Trinidad and Tobago, Barbados, Leeward Islands, and the Windward Islands. Students dedicated to

Windies cricket, but determined to attain a higher education at the same time, found an effective avenue.

Initially, Jeffrey Dujon was called upon to coach the CCC squad. Floyd Reifer soon assumed the role of player-coach and took the team to an impressive, competitive level. In short time, the CCC defeated all national teams and finally got the better of Jamaica. On three occasions it reached finals. Its credentials were established as a powerful force in regional cricket with a strong fan base.

The success of the CCC resided in its ability to produce dozens of players for national teams, and for Windies. CWI's policy stated that any student who established a positive performance reputation while playing for the CCC could subsequently be called upon to play for his national team; that is, a 'country first' principle was placed before the CCC defining it as an incubator for national and regional talent.

Within this context, the CCC produced national players and captains as well as the current Windies Test Captain, Jason Holder. The University was expected to provide leaders as well as players who could make a difference to Windies Test performance. The programme embraced this mandate and students came to see themselves as future Windies Test players. Formally educated, well disciplined, and effectively coached, their self-conception revolved around preserving and enhancing Windies Test in the global arena.

The final stage in laying the foundation for the rise of a twenty-first-century, competitive Test response was the establishment of a CWI–UWI Cricket Academy, built upon the foundations of the University's success, and the CCC as a transformational force. CWI's CEO, Ernest Hilaire, served as project leader. It was agreed to establish what was named the Sagicor–WICB High Performance Centre (HPC).

This was a seminal development in Windies Cricket. The Hunte-Hilaire regime moved swiftly to embrace the premises on which it was conceptualized. It was further agreed that the HPC would focus on inducting cricketers who were exiting the Under-19 team but not ready to transition to the Test or 'A' Team squads. It would, therefore, be the bridge between the 'youth' and 'senior' cultures – a space known to have an unacceptable level of high attrition.

These developments came together in the aftermath of the demised Shell Cricket Academy, led by legendary Windies cricket psychologist, Dr Rudi Webster, at the St Georges University in Grenada. Dr Webster, an architect in the Third Rising of West Indies Test Cricket, mental manager of Clive Lloyd's team in the late 1970s and early '80s, had created an academy programme for CWI that benefited many players. The ending of this project created a space that needed to be filled. The UWI, taking this circumstance into consideration, moved to strengthen its relations with Hunte's CWI with a view to partnering to create the academy project.

Players would enter the HPC on a semester basis as resident athletes. A programme of study and technical training was delivered over a three-month period. The objective was to produce a highly skilled cricketer who was academically equipped to manage a professional career, make rational choices, and commit to the advancement of Windies cricket while being a socially effective citizen. The programme was high performance based, with skills acquisition at the core surrounded by academic engagements and social enhancement programmes.

Sagicor Financial Corporation, on receiving formal presentations on the programme, agreed to be the principal sponsor. In short time, the HPC was having a substantial positive impact on Windies cricket. As a result, CWI brought its training and education programme in line with global best practices. What was available to male cricketers was also presented to females. The HPC became a hub of activity providing support for all teams, from Test to youth, males and females, as well as academic training for support staff.

As Chairman of the HPC Management Committee, project coordinator within the UWI network, and coordinator and academic advisor, I was well placed to report on the ways in which young cricketers benefited from the preparation received. Collectively, they committed to the Fourth Rising of Windies Test cricket, and saw the HPC as the vehicle that took them along the path of preparation.

Their exposure to the legends of the First Rising (Sir Everton and Sonny Ramadhin); the Second Rising (Sir Gary, Sir Wes, Lance Gibbs, Rohan Kanhai); and the Third Rising (Clive Lloyd, Viv Richards, Gordon Greenidge, Michael Holding, Desmond Haynes, and Andy Roberts) amongst others, transformed their consciousness. I monitored the depth of their determination to take Windies back to the top for a Fourth Rising.

The HPC was an effective technical and intellectual experience for a generation of cricketers who were prepared for the road ahead. Sadly, as the Julian Hunte regime at CWI gave way to the Dave Cameron presidency, the HPC was swiftly dismantled. There is no substitute for the HPC that took full advantage of the facilities of the UWI, both infrastructural and academic. Nor is there a replacement for the collective training of West Indian youth. The void is now a threat to the future, though mitigated to some extent by the legacy value of four cohorts of students who have benefited from the programme.

The UWI, then, for two decades, provided the critical support services for Windies Test cricket to rise. The message is now in full circulation. UWI, the messenger, remains fully engaged in other ways to educate, train and advocate. It represents a critical element in the structure of performance enhancement that will return Windies to the top of Test rankings. This is what Sir Frank expected of his UWI.

Receiving a bat with signatures of the Indian Team (2011) for the Centre of Cricket Research.

Sir Gary Sobers Indoor Cricket School, UWI, Cave Hill, Barbados (L to R) Tony Cozier, Lance Gibbs, author, Sir Gary Sobers, 2004

Ian Bishop speaking at the launch of the Sagicor-WICB High Performance Centre, UWI, Barbados, 2010

Launch of the Sagicor-WICB Cricket High Performance Centre, at UWI, Cave Hill Barbados, 2010. L to R: Sir Julian Hunte, President of WICB, Mrs Mara Thompson (wife) and Prime Minister of Barbados David Thompson, and Mr Dodridge Miller, President and CEO of Sagicor Financial Corporation

Congratulating Brian Lara (L) on receiving his honorary Degree (DLitt) from the UWI, St Augustine Campus, Trinidad and Tobago (2011)

The Sagicor-WICB Cricket High Performance Centre, Cave Hill Campus, UWI, Barbados

13

HOLDER'S HOPE: FINDING THE BALANCE

The media were precise in their choice of two headlines. They laid bare the bones of the issues that hold Windies cricket in limbo awaiting a new vision and purpose. The larger headline – both on the same page – screamed 'Holder must put WI first', and the other whispered 'Bravo leads Renegades' charge to victory.' How extraordinary that the biggest discourse in West Indies cricket could be so neatly contained on a single sport page. Few readers expected to find in such a place, a serious contribution to political ideology, the commentary on the nature of sovereignty, and the future of the West Indian nation.[1]

The Dwayne Bravo story focused on the activities of senior Windies players and their performances in the Australian T20 arena, while CWI sought to define the path leading to the next round of international engagements. Bravo's 'fine batting form' was identified as the basis of the Renegades victory over the Sidney Thunder. Scoring 47 runs off 24 deliveries Bravo was described as 'hammering' his team to victory, upstaging in the process, other Windies stars, Chris Gayle and Andre Russell. 'Big Bash' is celebrated in the detailed coverage of the performances, particularly those of the West Indians.[2]

The 'Holder' story relates to CWI asserting the 'Windies First' policy. Captain Jason Holder's request for leave from regional cricket duties in order to participate in the Pakistan Super League, which clashed with Windies first class championship, is presented as an example of 'players' choice in the age of globalization. There was no surprise that the young captain had made the request. News was already in circulation that he had indicated to CWI a prior desire to join the super league. CWI, in refusing a No-objection

Certificate to the captain, that would clear him to participate in the inaugural tournament, stated that his first priority needed to be the domestic competition. Holder was drafted in December 2015 by franchise team Quetta Gladiators but was unable to enter a contract agreement because of the WICB's position.

'The Captain,' said CWI, 'is among the retained players and has an obligation to participate in the domestic competition.' CWI had earlier warned top players 'to make themselves available' for these engagements in order to be 'eligible for selection to international tournaments'. CEO, Michael Muirhead, went to great lengths to emphasize that CWI locates domestic tournaments within the matrix of international events in order to facilitate players with global interests.[3]

Holder's compliance represented a declaration of his intention to lead Windies in Test, and to participate in all aspects of the team's rehabilitation. He is conscious of the crisis, in all its manifestations, and want to see the team move up in the international rankings. This perspective speaks to a developed understanding of the condition facing Windies. Few players, even of an older generation, understand the issue with the clarity that he does. There is a matured mentality at work and already he is building a reputation for sophisticated off-field analysis and communications.

There should be nothing phenomenal about this circumstance. Holder is a product of the cricket programme at The University of the West Indies, Cave Hill campus, in Barbados, where he is enrolled as a student. He has benefited from both the campus' cricket academy programme, as well as the Sagicor–WICB High Performance Centre (HPC).

As an intern, he received the formal tuition necessary for intellectual stimulation and growth, as well as the technical skills enhanced for performance. Tutors in the HPC programme spoke of his capacity for high-end thinking, and reported that he stood out within his cohort as a potential leader.

To observe Holder in conversation with Sir Gary and Sir Wes at the HPC was to witness a brilliant young mind hungry for practical knowledge and cricket wisdom. They, in turn, spoke of his sharp mind and amiable mentality, the qualities of a leader within, and beyond the boundary. At the campus, he trained and interacted with the student team that has evolved into the dominant national cricket force. Traditional clubs that produced the Windies legends such as Empire, Spartan, Wanderers, Maple, Pickwick and Police have had their historic reign ended by the students.

Holder has been a critical part of the University's cricket revolution. So too has Kraigg Brathwaite and Carlos Brathwaite, vice-captain of the Test team and captain of the 'A' team, respectively. They represent a new cohort of Windies cricketers – working class in origins, and matured within the campus environment before transitioning to Test and international cricket.

The meteoric rise of Holder is based, therefore, on a very solid foundation. His capacity speaks for itself. When, in 2013, he was ready to make his debut in CWI regional competition, it might have been fortuitous that Barbados did not select him to the national side. The reason for his non-selection was that the senior pacers were back for national duties – Fidel Edwards, Kemar Roach and Tino Best. With Sulieman Benn as the main spinner, and a few all-rounders thrown in, there was no room for Holder.

Fortunately, the Combined Campuses and Colleges (CCC) had access to him as a registered student. He was selected and made his regional debut. By the end of the season, he was recognized as a future Windies prospect. In all aspects of the game, his talent shone in a way not seen in recent years. He was immediately drafted to the Windies squad, and pursued by T20 franchises. While the University celebrated the achievement of its student, and was confident in his capacity to shift the paradigm at the leadership level, fear of premature captaincy duties lingered.

The reason for the reticence was obvious. Since the removal of Sammy from the captaincy there had been an obvious lowering of the expectation of its role and function. Gayle had rejected it as a burden too heavy to bear, and Sammy had relished the responsibility. The promotion of Denesh Ramdin and Bravo respectively met with resistance. The public understood and cried out for a display of more sophisticated reasoning.

Against this background, Holder stood out like the 6'5" colossus he is. A towering man with a corresponding cricket intellect, he presented himself as the logical choice for leadership. Clive Lloyd, chairman of selectors, saw it more clearly than most. Holder harkened back to the time of Lloyd and Viv Richards when a dedicated, committed consciousness understood the cause and purpose of the Windies enterprise. Lloyd could not contain his excitement. What was missing from the revival plan he was forging was leadership above and beyond the role of captaincy. In Holder he saw what Michael Holding had been calling for – a mind to manage the complexity of issues facing a team in decline. Lloyd went for it. He recommended the youth to captain Test and one day internationals (ODIs), while retaining Sammy for the T20 team. CWI endorsed the request and the rest is before us for judgement.

Lloyd's confidence was based on decades of discerning the appropriate mindset necessary for leadership. Since his own time at the helm, he has seen near a dozen captains come and go in very short time. In most instances, there were questions about their capacity to comprehend the problems, and lead towards resolution. Holder's sharp sense of the reality before him has helped his teammates whose respect for his thinking was quickly established.

Meanwhile, other legends lined up to respect the decisions to place Holder at the helm. Lara and Richards issued statements supportive of the young captain, and welcomed his leadership to clean up the debris that followed the removal of Gayle, Ramdin and Bravo. The bypassing of Samuels, arguably the most talented, through unreliable mercurial batsmen on the side, generated no discourse in the region. No one said he had been overlooked. Instead, there has been a calm realization that Holder has more of what it takes than any other player on the team.

Behind the Gayle 'give back' of the captaincy, is the capacity of Holder to stand up. There is no doubt that he comes to the role mentally prepared and technically ready. He speaks about his options with passion, and expresses his views on the resurrection of Windies. He was presented as a 'David' up against the Goliath of Test cricket.

The December 2015 Test tour to Australia was his grand beginning. Former cricketers from all nations watched the 'body' language of his team. Without saying explicitly they communicated that the 'old guard' refused to rise with performances. Tony Cozier quoted Ian Chappell's description of the decision to appoint him as 'ridiculous'. They described CWI as irrational and backward in its thinking to give 'the most difficult job in the game' to the 'youthful cricketer', and to 'burden him with a poor team'. Their shortsightedness was obvious. Holder's youth is accompanied by a developed character and matured intellect. His inexperience at the Test level is obvious, but the quality of his decision-making is in no way inferior to that of Lara, Carl Hooper, Courtney Walsh, Jimmy Adams, Ramdin and Bravo.[4]

There is also the matter of investing responsibility in the youth against the backdrop of the failure of elders. The data speaks for itself. The team failed miserably under the captaincy of older, more experienced players, who not only turned out dismal personal performances but brought Windies into disrepute by their industrial actions and media musings. In every way, then, Holder seemed superior to those before in respect of captaincy and leadership. Critically, his presence sends a powerful developmental message to the Caribbean community.[5]

The contradiction in the Cozier–Chappell posture was revealed in their admission that there was a 'glaring' lack of support for Holder from senior players, those 'who need a kick up the backside'.

Chappell, noted Cozier, was referring to Marlon Samuels, Jerome Taylor, and Kemar Roach. Samuels, it is said, 'loitered around the outfield in Hobart, showing little interest in the proceedings' and 'occasionally, he donned his designer sunglasses, and occasionally broke into a casual trot in pursuit of the ball.'[6]

Finally, came the absurdity of Mark Nicholas. 'The most feasible, if disturbing, answers to Windies decline,' he said, 'is the separate territories that have banded together for over 100 years. There is an inevitable demise in their Test game and maybe there should be a concentration solely on the shorter formats,' he concluded. Nicholas took this diatribe to its logical distortion with a series of racist rants strung together as an argument about the future of Windies. After describing the years of the Lloyd–Richards dominance as a 'fluke', he stated that one should go to the Caribbean and:

> Be delighted by the simple life. Fewer than six million people, and endearing lack of infrastructure, no compelling reason for investment outside its own boundaries – except tourism, of course, and low levels of motivation for much but sun, sea, sand, and those glorious sunsets. Wonderful! May it forever be so.[7]

Further derogatory comments ended with the idea that 'perhaps it now makes more sense for the regions to go it alone.'[8] Then came his 'crying shame' for Holder:

> One cannot help but feel for Holder, who has been sent to the wolves as much because of a lack of options as anything else. He is a promising cricketer trying to make his way in three formats of a complex and widely profiled game. His standards are high and his dignity unimpeachable. But the captaincy, though a great honour, is surely a burden.[9]

None of this shows any kind of understanding of Caribbean society and cricket beyond the superficial and the mundane. He illustrates what is clearly a T20 kind of writing about complex matters. Holder is not carrying a burden of leadership for the poor and downtrodden. He was socially created for this role at this time. He was trained within the UWI academy for the task, and like any other form of alignment he is comfortable with the cause for which he was created. Not to understand this is to reside outside the Caribbean ontological environment.

Whether Holder should lead within the moment of crisis is irrelevant. What is important is that he is supported conceptually by the global backlash against the market mentality of senior Windies stars who have turned their backs on Test obligations. The resentment is growing everywhere, starting at home and finding traction among fans of many nations. There is a strong current against Windies globetrotters and freelancers, and it is within this approaching storm that Holder is held up. There are forces at work that have made his load easier to lift. A counter-culture is coming and Holder is the hero of the emerging agenda.

Much of this finds no footage within the journalistic outpouring about persistent Windies gloom. Holder, therefore, is now the most misunderstood cricketer in the Caribbean, if not in world cricket. He will be elevated rather than sucked down by these counter-cultural forces. They will give him the wind he needs for his wings, and pundits will experience what is really not a paradox but an analysis of sociological currents operating within a critique of globalization as a failed development model.

To hold up Holder, therefore, in the manner that Lloyd has, and the WICB imagined, is to recognize that the world on the surface is not all that there is; and to dwell there is not to discern structures and strata that move from time to time to create a new order. Holder is the hero of the new order that has matured quietly in the bosom of the decay that followed the 'dollar first principle' of the Gayle generation.

Holder is, furthermore, the logical mind of the Caribbean coming to terms with an internal critique of the prior order that has been gradually discredited as not in the interest of the many. Having made up its mind about what is best for Windies, the public moved swiftly to endorse Lloyd's choice because it sees a mind capable of doing what needs to be done. It sees a young man willing to stand against the rising tide, pointing towards higher ground.

The evidence suggests that Holder is the harbinger, calling for the return of Caribbean sense and sensibility to the centre of its own story. Washed along by the current of cash, the community now sees that the culture of Test is at stake, and that its 100-year-old investment is at risk of being written off as bad debt. Holder is propelled into the space to specify the new parameters for his cohort, those mostly socialized in the criticisms of the abandonment of nation in the flames of the franchise.

The Cozier–Chappell–Nicholas treatise that invites the fragmentation of the Windies into little windows through which each community sees the world not only falls flat on the clayed feet of political illiteracy, but it does not comprehend the power of education to confront despair. Holder does not speak, unlike Lara, about the 'guys coming from different countries' who are hard to harness into a unified force. This is not his makeup. This explains why Nicholas speaks of his emergence from the Wanderers Club in Barbados, Cozier's Club, which for almost a century was the whites-only, apartheid bastion, of Bajan cricket.

But to ask Holder of his greatest anxiety is to begin a conversation that connects his consciousness to an analysis of resources and resilience at the performance base of Windies. He speaks about professional motivation, the search for excellence at the crease, and the capacity of his comrades to believe in their ability to improve at a rate faster than their competitors. He is calling upon them to climb a steeper growth curve, and to do so in the way that former players did. That is, he recognizes that maturity matters most. He is the latest model long perfected by captains the likes of Frank Worrell, Garfield Sobers, Clive Lloyd, and Vivian Richards. He will rally to his cause a cohort of committed youth steeped in the post-Gayle counter-cultural context.

The perception, then, that Holder is a John the Baptist, 'lost' in the wilderness, is misplaced. He is keenly aware of where he stands and the direction of his destiny. He stands against the notion of West Indian helplessness and the pathetic parade of condescending journalism that calls to question the capacity of Caribbean civilization to cure its own ills. 'Jason Holder', they tell us, 'is crying out for support from all quarters as he finds himself in an unenviable role'.

Furthermore, we are told:

> With people in the Caribbean repulsed by the consistently deteriorating performance from a shambolic West Indies outfit, the International Cricket Council (ICC) needs to step in and reinvigorate a major draw card. A composite of tiny islands that laid down the gauntlet and demolished every opponent in sight to establish one of sport's greatest streaks during the '80s now evokes constant ridicule and disdain. The team which went through a staggering 31 Test series without being conquered from April 1980 to March 1995 is struggling to compete for the full length of a Test match.[10]

Holder's presence, it is recognized, cannot turn the tide. The primary reason why the 'big names' are not playing Tests for their country, says the reporter, 'is the burgeoning money on offer'. The ICC is seen as having the solution to the situation in which Windies cannot bring its 'maroons' back into the fold. It should devise a strategy to redirect a larger share of the global revenue into CWI in order to guarantee 'better monetary benefits for the beleaguered cricketers'. Furthermore, the narrative goes, the ICC should insist that Windies grassroots game is better funded in order to steer potentials away from 'athletics and basketball'. An investment in sports education would also ensure that 'the next generation of flamboyant islanders' would become more 'aware of the rich heritage of their ancestors'. This is the help Holder is said to be in need of if he is to 'reawaken the sleeping giants from what has been a really long slumber.'[11]

These recommendations are well taken, but behind them resides a matrix of political considerations of which the captain is fully aware. Only the loyalty of Windies players to the cause can stem the tide that is ripping apart the beaches. Here is where Holder's destiny lies.

West Indian society must take a united stance that players, nurtured in the youth tournaments of the region, on reaching senior status must dedicate their core energy to the cause of Windies.

CWI alone cannot assure this. This 'country first' norm which exists in Australia, India, South Africa, England, and indeed all the Test playing countries, must be implemented in Windies. The conversation in the region about 'citizen before society' must be addressed and the ideology eradicated. It will be Test cricket today and everything else tomorrow.

The lightspirited declaration of loyalty to Windies issued by Gayle and Bravo especially, should be set aside as a cynical disregard of the future of Windies cricket. These players who were 'big bashing' in Australia as Holder's Test men stood bravely in the face of a battering battalion with ballistic missiles illustrated the cowardice of the cash and carnival option they chose in venues within an eye's view. There was no shame but endless pride in Holders' acceptance of the truth of this situation. He spoke calmly about the need to offer a better financial package for his young Test cricketers. This is just the beginning. He knows only too well that at the moment they might not be deemed deserving in the public's eye, but the time will come.

Lara read the wicket correctly in his assessment of Holder's captaincy in all formats of the game as a landmark appointment for Caribbean cricket. He was entirely satisfied that the captain has all the prerequisites 'to lead Caribbean cricket to great heights'. Lara gave him a ten year ticket, and made reference to South Africa's brilliant, insightful appointment of an equally young Graeme Smith as captain. The comparison is indeed striking. Smith went on to become his country's most successful captain, performing superbly over a long and brilliant career.[12]

Already, Holder has shown his matured grasp of the contextual issue. Chris Barratt asserted that Holder's team, on the 2015 tour of Australia, 'all earn less than even the lowest-paid members of the Australian team'. This observation generated a comment from the captain. He joined with discarded England player Kevin Pieterson in calling upon 'the ICC to bankroll contracts for Test players around the world to ensure they are not lost to Twenty 20 cricket.' He declared the paramountcy of two fundamental principles: first, that 'country must come first'; second, that a balance between national representation and players' income maximization strategies must be established within a culture of dialogue and development.[13]

The captain spoke to a new vision for Windies renovation and restoration: He noted:

> Obviously we're in a situation where the money isn't great for us at the moment and we've been in numerous battles for that but that's beyond our control at the present time…I think we need to strike a balance, and I'm not knocking T20 cricket because I love T20 cricket myself, but we just need to find a way where the country comes first and then we are flexible in terms of allowing people to make money outside of international cricket. I don't think we should be playing hardball and deny people from going and playing, but there has to be a situation where the country comes first and then we are flexible in terms of allowing people to make money outside of international cricket. I think once we get to the stage the players will buy in.[14]

As a principle driven leader, Holder clearly grasps the macroeconomic issues involved in terms of the relative financial poverty of the Caribbean. His call for flexibility addresses the issue of capacity to pay, given that cricketers, like all Caribbean professionals, are not compensated at the same level as their global counterparts. He 'knows only too well,' says Barratt 'about the gulf in earning capacity not only between the Australians and the West Indies but also between his teammates and Gayle and Co…,' but he has remained focused on his task, even in the face of criticisms about his inexperience.[15]

14

EMPIRE EXPOSED: THE NERVE OF NICHOLAS!

Windies Test cricket will rise again, and when it does it will be as James Baldwin said in 1963, the 'fire next time'. Windies youth are rewinding. Hostile critics, like Mark Nicholas, cannot read the trends. This led him to conclude that 'there's little hope of things improving the way they're going at the moment.' The poverty of perception is not surprising. The Caribbean world is grossly misunderstood and more often than not conclusions such as those of Nicholas become notorious and serve as manifestos of naysayers.

Nicholas attempted to deal Windies players, and their social culture, a dastardly low blow. He went beyond bat and ball in his caustic commentary and, by implication, issued a proclamation that sought to burn to ashes all Windies had achieved in 100 years of Test and international cricket. As a former player who claimed intimate friendship with the legendary Malcolm Marshall and familiarity with Viv Richards and Joel Garner, his dismissal of Windies intellectual capacity and achievement went beyond the border of disdain. 'It is difficult to see a resurrection,' he said. 'The years of plenty were something of a fluke, as if the stars aligned to produce something astrologers will talk about for all time; a momentary thing of beauty and brilliance and, within it, an irresistible brutality.'[1]

It is not necessary to address his 'Fluke Theory' of Windies achievement. The denigration involved in his denouncement is evident given the attitude he possesses as one from a privileged environment who did not extract from it a personal proficient performance when it was his turn at the crease. He was never a high performer for England when it mattered. He was missing from the middle when the heat was on.

There was no finer collection of players in the world that combined to create the first rising of Windies. The 3Ws – Frank Worrell, Everton Weekes and Clyde Walcott – were undoubtedly the best middle order on earth, and Sonny Ramadhin and Alf Valentine the spin twins, devastated teams in a manner unprecedented. England's best men, with all the literacy in their upbringing, could not read them in the air or off the turf. The barely literate Ramadhin made a fool of men schooled in England's finest universities. With reliable openers in Allan Rae and Jeffrey Stollmeyer, and a legacy that now included George Headley and Learie Constantine, Windies had risen within and beyond the boundary to a place hitherto reserved for the Anglo–Australian alliance.

The audacity of Windies in 1951 to challenge the Aussies in a showdown for the world title also attracted the racist attention of the anthropologically fossilized, who considered the team too big for its boots – a familiar concept that connotes fear of the colonial. After 20 years at the bottom, the team rose up and threatened to grip Australia by the throat, but lacked the tenacity to hold on and tighten.

The result was an instructive thrashing that served to strengthen the team. Back to the valley they tumbled, and after residing there for another 15 years, rose up for the second time in the 1960s. This second rising under Worrell and Sobers was ferocious. All were brushed aside in short time – England by Worrell in 1963, and between 1965 and 1967 the Indians, England again, and the Aussies were put to the sword by Sobers. In 1967, Windies were the top Test team in the world. The second rising was the Worrell–Sobers revolution that Nicholas might not have studied in school, but should show familiarity as a cricket writer.

The rise from the bottom to the top was bold, beautiful, and brilliant. It was not predicted by English pundits, neither was it seen coming by the Aussies. The defeat by England in 1968 ended the sojourn at the top. But it was the first conquest of Everest that was important. It was a Moses moment. Windies had seen the Promised Land, and though they did not set up shop there and take possession, they knew what was there and how to get back. From the top they tumbled, once again to the bottom, where they resided for a decade – retooling, rewinding, rethinking and finding energy for the third rising. When it did, it came in the form of Clive Lloyd's legions that were to become the greatest legends of the game now redefined and remade in their own image.

The Third Rising was 'Fire In Babylon'. Windies, having gone to the top and seen the lay of the land, now lingered, and reveled in the view for two decades. The lessons of these journeys seem lost on the peddlers of doom and gloom, many of whom were players – now pundits – who had been at the long end of the Windies stick. Many remained in shock, post dramatically, from the awe of Windies' blistering batsmen and pulverizing pacers. The evidence of this syndrome is to be found in the literature and commentary that set out the current litany of Windies woe! The instinct to punish Windies for what was done to them as players persists. The landscape of the mind, as it seeks to transcend trauma, is not a terrain easily conquered.

And so Windies have fallen, once again, from the top. There is nothing new about this. The significance of Nicholas's 'fluke theory', then, is that it lacks understanding of the history of Windies cricket, and not only denies the intellectual and strategic capacity of the team to fix their challenges, but to change the status quo. Furthermore, he brushes aside the internal logic of the Windies game as it relates to transformation cycles in Caribbean society, a relationship well documented in the literature of the region.[2]

The notion that West Indians, somehow, stumbled into history and found a niche which they grabbed like mindless monsters – hence the frequent use of the word 'brutal' to describe their success – has roots deep within the narratives of English racism. The anti-colonial black, rising up from slavery, was always the 'brute'; the oppressive, dehumanizing, genocidal colonizer was somehow the gentleman dispensing justice. Furthermore, the idea that the native could possibly have a more developed intellectual and strategic insight and practice has to be denied and detonated. Surely this is the basis of the 'fluke theory' that suggests an act of cosmic alignment rather than community commitment. This, tragically, is why the racial rant of Nicholas went largely unnoticed until Darren Sammy, in his T20 victory speech in 2016, called him out and drew his apology.

The black world had heard it all before. The pyramids in Egypt were not built by Africans. Such a colonized set of creatures, how could this be? There were no such magnificent structures in Europe. England had a few ruins left behind by transitory Romans, some of which have inspired spiritual ritual and offer revelations to the religious. But since there is no evidence of Europeans as pyramid builders, they must have been made by aliens. The alignment of the stars, says Nicholas, created a real life phenomenon that came into being in 1978 in the West Indies and lasted for near two decades. No one should, therefore, expect another such galactic event in our lifetime.

Nicholas, unfortunately, has ignored the earthly cricketing history of his own nation – England. The record shows that notwithstanding the legacy capacity of the British Empire, including its grand imperial and political performance culture as a metropole, its international cricket credential had collapsed in the early 1970s. For 20 years, England remained in the bottom section of Test cricket ranking. The West Indians were not the only ones to bring English cricket to shame. By the mid-1980s, it appeared that every team that came to the country took advantage of their low vantage level. It was a painful period for English cricket fans, officials, and players. The team appeared inept, lacking in skill and fortitude. All that is said today about Windies and CWI was attributed to the MCC – an acronym that meant for some 'making cricket comedy'.

India, for example, was not an elite Test team in the 1980s, yet England struggled to get the better of them. In the 1979 tour to India, England etched out a 1-0 victory, with three Tests drawn; in the 1981/2 series in India, they went down 1-0, with 5 Tests drawn; in 1982, in England, again they etched out a marginal 1-0 victory, with 2 Tests drawn; in the 1984/85 tour to India, another narrow victory, 2-1, with two Tests drawn; in the 1986 tour to England, the visitors climbed above and defeated the host 2-0 with 1 Test drawn; and in the 1990 home series, again England scraped home 1-0 with two Tests drawn. Finally, in the 1992–93 visit to India, the host finally sealed England's fate with a 3-0 'brown-wash'.

By the 1990s, Australia was piling on the pain upon a clearly demoralized England set up. English fans turned away from their national team in disgust.

Cricket stands were generally 60 per cent empty for home series, so alienated the nation had become. The BBC in response to the loss of national interest moved to abandon 'free to air' televising of Test cricket in the country.

The critical indicator of England's fall, however, was its bowling. After a decade of apprenticeship, Sri Lanka, the new kid on the Test block, took them on. The first Test in 1981/82, England won against the rookies, but by the time of the second series in 1984, Sri Lanka was putting England to the sword in the one Test match which was played at Lords.

T:5 1990s – England vs. Australia Test Series Results

Date	Australia	England
1989	4	0
1990/91	3	0
1993	4	1
1994/5	3	1
1997	3	2
1998/99	3	1
2001	4	1

Scoring 434/4 declared, with S. Wettimuny hammering bowlers all over the park in a massive 190, and L. Mendis as support also crafting a polished century, they bowled out England for 370, and then moved on to declare at 294 for 7 (S. Silva 102). Time ran out upon the rising visitors. Then, in the 1992/93 series, Sri Lanka defeated England and repeated it in 1998. Even a minnow had gotten the better of the mighty.

The significance of this was evident. The once all conquering England, home of the game, definer of the code, were incapable of imposing their will on the field, and had crashed to the bottom. The media made mincemeat of teams that were 'blackwashed' by the Windies, humbled by the Aussies, and then, finally, trampled on by the new arrivants, Sri Lanka.

England became synonymous with poor, unsustainable cricket. All eyes looked upon empty stands as the game seemed a relic of the past. The national Test game was pronounced dead in the Thames. It was over, and Shirley Bassey was singing. But with the turn of the century, after 20 years as an 'also ran team', England found its groove and regained its gravitas. The 2005 double Ashes victories over Australia signalled the evidence of the renaissance, which was 20 years in the making.

Post-Gayle

Nicholas's 'Fluke thesis' aside, conceptual and actual preparations are emerging to lay the foundation for the 'Fourth Rising' in Windies Test performance. A new cadre of players is being honed in the formal system of national academies, as well as in the UWI network. There is obviously a pressing need to empower these systems with sustainable strategies.

Currently, the CCC programme that has delivered Jason Holder and Carlos Brathwaite, and many other younger players to professional careers, is the region's most advanced training system. Its players are found in all national teams. They have a distinct identity and special qualities in terms of cognitive capacity on and off the field. A new player ethos is emerging, one that is more amenable to the high-end professional preparation required for Test cricket.

The decision by CWI, UWI and Sagicor to build upon this template was the positive development needed to lay the foundation for the Fourth Rising. The HPC was the key element in the imagined future. Its role was to re-centre cricketers' consciousness, and to establish the framework for the restoration of the 'Windies First' policy. Sadly, CWI has abandoned the HPC in its stride.

The rise of an academy cohort in the aftermath of the Gayle–Bravo–Ramdin regimes represents a break from the unfocused, decentred, and non-committed consciousness that emerged from the WIPA's leadership agenda and style. These youths are in tune with Holder's call for balance in the multiple options they face while holding to the 'country first' principle. As the Test team grows in its reliance upon these younger players, who are less easily manipulated by erratic, anti-development industrial relations actions, the stronger it will be as a contending force. The path is well prepared for this transition that will transform the team into a knowledge and learning operation.

The defeat of the corrosive consciousness of the past decade that culminated in team walk-out against Bangladesh, and the walk-off in India, suggests a break with the mentality that sucked the spirit and sold the soul of Windies. Young, emerging HPC-trained players are not made of the same material that snubbed President Mandela in 1998, and they that took pride in driving CWI into bankruptcy with industrial strife. Neither will they support a strategy to subvert Windies cricket with a view to taking over its operations in a management coup.

They are more likely to see through and dismiss the schemes concocted in aspects of Dinanath Ramnarine's WIPA's ethos, elements of which continue to see other stakeholders of the game as lesser than rather than equal to its own identity. The political leadership of the region is now required to assist in strengthening this new approach rather than subvert its core with parochial pressures. Players in flight from the discipline of CWI find solace in the culture of national politics. The perception that political pressure 'back home', in their 'nation', is a safety net in the aftermath of their anti-regional choices has been a major source of division.

The recent calls upon the political leadership of the region to settle player-board disputes have had the effect of strengthening player belief that CWI is injurious of their interests. While it is possible to comprehend how perceptions of their vulnerability in the face of the CWI's solidarity can shape players judgment, the narratives emerging from these consultations have strengthened their conviction that CWI is not a fair and ethical employer.

With media support growing for this opinion, the institutional authority and status of CWI fell dramatically, damaging its ability to function effectively. The good news is that much of this is changing as some politicians have come to realize that all was not above board with much of the WIPA's posturing and polemics.

The hyped hysteria within the players' ranks, a consequence of the public rhetoric of Ramnarine's leadership especially, inhibited players' capacity to perform where it mattered most, on the field of play. The carrying of emotional baggage from the boardroom to the field has resulted in the obvious display of nonchalance. While this manner of managing differences and conflict is to be expected, the new cohort of players makes distinctions with greater ease and less drama. In general, there has been an improvement in the professional conduct of the team even within the context of industrial relations tensions. The Holder approach is the beginning of a new environmental engineering.

Critically, there has been a cessation in the outpouring of antipathy in the relations between 'legends' and 'losers'. The most destructive aspect of Windies fall from dominance has been the unleashing of mutual hostility between these groups. The legends have been brutal in their bashing of the 'losers' who appeared to them casual, careless, and generally cavalier about their extraordinary inheritance. Some comments have struck the heart of young players with long-term crippling effect.

Undoubtedly, the West Indian preference for looking cool on the outside while frost eats away at the inside, had not always been catered for in the widespread condemnation. This has been unfortunate. In response, the 'losers' have sought to devalue the legacy by intimating that 'back then' the competition was less intense than today. It became a norm, for example, for young batsmen to speak of the slowness of opposition pace in the '70s and '80s in comparison with their time. They also speak about the lesser quality of batsmen who faced up to the '80s Windies pace quartet. The objective of these assertions was self-protection from the changes laid against them.

Much of the 'mutually assured destruction' (MAD) that typified the generational meltdown began in the two decades after 1995. Michael Holding did receive some push back for his acerbic critique of Brian Lara as irresponsible, and Ramdin is still 'in the doghouse' for his 'tek that' public slam of Sir Viv, but there have been many others that have shaped 'legend-losers' relations.

By 2000, 'freeze' was felt in many places where the two groups assembled. Each group took to opposite sides leaving the middle occupied by guests who formed a human shield. The complete breakdown in communication between two generations did considerable damage to an already deteriorating circumstance. While it represented an obvious recoil from what is best practice in a learning fraternity, there was also the feeling that it was a long-term circumstance. For over ten years, the legends traded comments in the traditional print media. The 'losers' used other modern forms to shield themselves, and ripped apart the reputations of elders within the electronic echelon. Social media, for example, became the place of the face-off.

This cannibalism has abated under Holder's regime, largely as a result of his obvious effort to change the conversation and bring the assets of legends into the camp. The wholesale acceptance of his leadership is a sure sign that there is a campaign for the integration of the generations. He has called upon legends to lend support in critical spaces, such as the nets, locker room and over dinner tables. A semblance of normalcy has been restored in the relations between the heroes of Second and Third Risings. This aspect of the preparation for the Fourth Rising is well on its way and already positively impacting attitude and field results.

Holder's young players have received structured seminars on these eruptions, featuring the phenomenal contributions of legends. Their formal exposures to the legacy place them in a position to understand, respect, and celebrate. The rally around Holder's squad by legends constitutes a radical revision of the narrative.

Lloyd was well positioned to lead the healing. The 'mind game' is gradually being fixed as young talent is nurtured in academies. The UWI has thrown its full support behind the rising youth. Greater care is being taken of the new crop, and the signs of resilience are evident. The alignment of legends with this ethos, and with the higher education system playing its part, the social environment of Windies international cricket is being radically transformed. The 'walk outs', and 'walk offs', will be a thing of the past, and the relations between players and management will be driven by the imperatives of greater sophistication.

The decision by the post-Ramnarine WIPA, in 2015, to reach out to the UWI and to sign a Memorandum of Understanding for the further and specific education and training of cricketers is a logical outgrowth of these developments. Principal of the Open Campus, Dr Luz Longsworth, has created an online portal to be buttressed with face-to-face teaching and learning. For the first time, Windies cricketers will exist within the 'learning networks' of globally accessible education and training.

The aggressive 'money first' policy that typified Ramnarine's WIPA regime was a major force that determined the poor performance culture within the Windies camp. It destroyed the semblance of a 'value for money' relationship with performance; it ignored issues relevant to CWI capacity to pay. Benchmarking against some of the wealthiest economies in the world might be good in principle, but as it is unattainable in practice it led to anger, disillusionment and a spirit of despair within the locker room.

The call for balance by Holder will serve to energize and refocus players who are now in a position to think for themselves. They are not prepared to blindly follow Ramnarine's element within the WIPA whose primary agenda was not to empower players and sustain excellence in the Windies, but to discredit and destroy CWI in order to take control of Windies cricketers, and, by extension, the running of West Indies cricket. Neither will they be easily won by any CWI's short term, anti-player postures and policies.

Ramnarine's agenda to take over Windies cricket was skilfully concealed beneath layers of industrial relations unrests that were systemically sponsored and stoked. Using the guise of acting for the good of cricketers, the WIPA under Ramnarine, effectively mobilized supportive media, and unleashed a reign of doubt and division within the cricket fraternity. Anyone who opposed this agenda was declared an enemy of cricketers. Anyone who informed the WIPA that it had gone too far in their scorched-earth policy was branded an ally and apologist of CWI.

President Wavell Hinds' recent recognition that the 'coup' had been foiled now signals the dawn of a return to the original mandate of the organization – to use its resources, working with stakeholders, for the advancement of cricketers and Windies cricket in general. This realization came in the aftermath of Dwayne Bravo's team walk out in India. Bravo blamed Hinds for selling out his teammates to CWI, and using the resources of elite cricketers to fund players down the pipeline. Marlon Samuels's declaration that WIPA and

Hinds could not represent him, and that he wanted no part of the walk out, was a throwback to the spirit of disaffection built up by Ramnarine's regime.

The apparent stabilization of the WIPA, and its attempt at recuperation under Hinds, is an enormous gain for Windies. The reinvention of the WIPA will represent the final undoing of the Ramnarine ethos that had strived on excessive conflict, unthinking policy aggression, and the creation of a doomsday scenario within the culture of cricket. While for some observers a cancer had taken root within the industrial relations body of Windies cricket, it is now evident under the 'new style WIPA' the body is in remission, and prospects for a healthy future seem assured.

Allied to the process has been the discourse surrounding future governance models for Windies cricket. A document, 'The Report of a Committee on Governance of West Indies Cricket', was submitted to the WICB and CARICOM in 2007. The Committee was chaired by the Most Honourable P.J. Patterson, the distinguished former Prime Minister of Jamaica, and included Sir Alister McIntyre, former Vice Chancellor of the UWI and outstanding development economist, and the distinguished writer, Dr Ian McDonald. Now known as the Patterson Report, it represents the guiding vision for the rehabilitation of the WICB and Windies Test cricket in the twenty-first century.[3]

The Patterson Report performed four fundamental tasks within the rethinking strategy for the Fourth Rising. First, it demonstrated that Caribbean intellectuals, public leaders and persons of high quality in respect of commitment to civic society are standing firmly behind Windies cricket, and are prepared to do all they can to revive it as a public good. Second, it said that the Caribbean as a learning society has within it all the necessary intellectual and strategic competencies to conceptualize and chart the rebirth of Windies Test cricket. Third, it said that there must be precise reading of the past and accurate conception of the future to inform the core of

decision making. Fourth, it showed that Caribbean society is willing
to mobilize the highest levels of respected leadership available to act
on its behalf for the presentation of its greatest, collective cultural
achievement – Windies Test cricket.

CWI accepted and respected the core concepts of the report, but
could not readily agree to a specific recommendation – the creation
of a stakeholders Council to which the President of CWI would
report on his/her stewardship. The Board, under President Julian
Hunte's leadership, implemented at least 80 per cent of the report's
recommendation, but could not go forward with the Council as an
authoritative body over CWI. While Hunte was prepared to accept
a stakeholder's Council as advisor to the President and the board,
media discourse suggested that the report has been dismissed in its
totality.

The public conversation in this regard has been largely inaccurate.
The Patterson Report became a blueprint for reform on many fronts,
but the insistence that CWI should be held to account by a body
other than itself became a stumbling block around the question of
governance. Patterson, acting in the best interest of Windies Cricket,
and with the full backing of the Caribbean people, rightfully called
for full accountability as a matter of principle. CWI called for
compromise, and appointed a number of 'non-aligned', independent
directors – persons from industry, academia, commerce, finance
and sport to broaden and strengthen representation and the spirit
of accountability.

Critically, the Patterson Report stands as a beacon for the best
of what the West Indies can be in that it declared the relevant
'quality values' of transparency, accountability, and regionality,
as the pertinent principles for the re-emergence of Windies Test
cricket. Only the best and most appropriate governance can take the
Windies forward, the report insisted. Countries like England and
Australia that have modernized their mandates and governance have
all done well. The logic of the Patterson Report is as compelling as
it is impeccable.

The power and persuasion implicit in the contribution of the Patterson Report, furthermore, is to be found in the mobilization of public opinion. The conversation created has proven that West Indian people are not prepared to allow their Test cricket to remain as a shadow of its former self. The public has spoken, and Mr Patterson has written. There is now a Caribbean consensus that governance reform must and will guide the strategic planning to empower the Holder era. With fit for purpose governance, a WIPA development agenda in place, a captain that understands complexity and seeks to find balance, in addition to public critique and support, the context for a Windies Fourth Rising is now in place.

The rebuilding process has begun. Sammy did show what needed to be done. He was a change agent but surrounded by the remnants of the older order, and its powerful allies, he was removed from the captaincy on spurious grounds that camouflage the campaign to roll back the agenda. The failure of the Ramdin–Bravo regimes was predictable, but it opened the door for real change. The decks are now cleared and a new dispensation within the team is in place. CWI gave Lloyd a free hand to craft the ideological environment of a 'Windies First' regime. The year 2020 is symbolic, not because of the Windies continued competitiveness of the T20 format of the game, but because it is the year in which they will return to the upper room.

15

PREPARING FOR THE FOURTH RISING

February 14, 2016, was a 'back to the future' moment in Windies Cricket. The Windies under-19 squad seemed focused and dignified in its approach to the T20 World Cup while the senior players were bargaining for more cash and credit at the beginning of their T20 World Cup.

It was more than a tale of two cups. It was the reality of two teams at the extreme ends of the ideological spectrum. Hearing different drums, they were dancing to the divergent beat of 'more dollars' and 'Windies First'. One part of the dance hall was filled with the aura of the 'more pay' issue, and another vibrated with the vision of youth hell-bent on beating Bangladesh and injuring India on the way to establishing world T20 dominance.

The Under-19 team did win the World Cup by beating tournament favourites India by a significant margin of five wickets in Dhaka, Bangladesh. It was a phenomenal performance that saw the youth rise with maturity in the humid sub-continent environment that was new to most and never kind to any. They hijacked highflying India with a superior ground game. There should have been no surprises. They had been on a winning streak over the past two years, losing not a single one day international (ODI) since 2014. Yet, the pundits and punters had written them down and off!

Rejecting the reasoning that all was lost, Windies youths won the toss and inserted the Indians. This was an action indicating an upsurge of confidence and conviction that was to take them to victory. Windies Test and ODI captain Jason Holder, recognizing the significance of the commitment of the youth, declared his joy. 'What a team!' he exclaimed; 'these guys showed the depth and balance of their side. They stuck together in tough times and now can celebrate this moment. I am a proud West Indian today,' he said, 'and we must celebrate this wonderful achievement as these guys have done a lot for our region.'[1]

Meanwhile, back in a more familiar territory, the senior T20 squad was preparing to regain a title they won in 2012 and lost in 2014. They began as was predicted – with a public display of acrimony over money and management. Captain Darren Sammy, like Captain Bravo before him, was the principal spokesman for the disgruntled squad. In rejecting the terms and conditions offered for the tour by CWI, Sammy's song was sorrow to a public wishing to hear of victories rather than read of the venom in vexing industrial relations.

In a letter to CWI, on behalf of his men, Sammy stated that they 'can't accept' what they interpreted as 'huge financial reductions' in the terms of their contracts. The comparison was made in respect of the previous ICC tournaments. He made reference to an 80 per cent cut in tour income, and called upon CWI to 'address this urgently'. Behind the broadside was the usual rhetoric intended to contextualize the content of the threat. 'We want to represent the West Indies,' he said, 'but the financials on offer we can't accept.'[2]

Sammy's gauntlet was sharpened with references to ICC's financial relations to CWI. 'Obviously,' he said, 'I am not privy to exact numbers paid to the WICB from the ICC, but I understand US$8m will be paid to the Board.' 'Traditionally,' he said, '25% has been paid to the squad. That would equate to US$2m, therefore, approximately US$133,000 per player.' He added: 'worst case scenario the squad would earn $414,000 collectively under the terms of the contract offered by WICB to participate in the T20 World Cup 2016. That is just over 5% – a staggering difference, near 80% reduction.'[3]

The captain went on to identify signs of distrust in all things around him. Team members do not trust the WICB, he indicated, it refuses to offer them a fair deal, and there is an endemic belief that they are being exploited. Furthermore, he said, '14 of the 15-man squad are not a part of WIPA, and therefore, had not given the organization the authority to negotiate on the behalf.' The players' rejection of the WIPA is linked to the belief that the representative body had capitulated to CWI, a position affirmed by Bravo who led the walk off in India. Rejecting both CWI and the WIPA, the Sammy Team opted to stand alone as sole arbiter of its interests.[4]

CWI's reaction to players' demands was predictably swift and swinging. It denounced the calculations of the captain as 'totally incorrect' and fictional. The fantasy figures, said Michael Muirhead, CEO of CWI, have no basis in any recognizable calculation, and bear no relations to any reasoning relevant to the ICC's financial methodology. Furthermore, he said, WIPA is recognized by CWI as the bargaining unit for all players whether they accept it or not. Sammy was put in his place in an aggressive fashion. The team was told by its employer to sign up or stand down and be replaced. In short time, the news sprinted around the region that players had given their employer the pleasure of their legal compliance.

Windies seniors did go on to win the 2016 tournament and were celebrated across and within the region, as were the Under-19 team. It was the first time both teams had won these respective ICC titles. The teens' team had been consistent since the championship was inaugurated in 1988. There had been a ten year break in the tournament, and with its resumption in 1998, 16 teams have contested. Windies did not win before 2016, but placed third in 1988, fifth in 2000, fourth in 2002, second in 2004, and third in 2010. Australia and India have both won the title three times, Pakistan twice, and England and South Africa, once. Both New Zealand and Sri Lanka made it to the finals without winning. It is also instructive to note that in the 1998 contests Chris Gayle had scored 364 runs, the most for the tournament.

The young Windies won, said Mohammad Islam, with a 'mix of high-speed hustle with the ball and patience with the bat'. These are characteristics long associated with the overall Windies brand, but his admission that the team 'didn't drop their intensity' struck home as a rare report within recent years.[5] The teens' commitment, and focus were evident in the semi-final when they successfully chased 227 against the home team, in the presence of 10,000 fans at the Sher-e-Bangla Stadium. They got home with three wickets to spare. It was a spectacular victory; a magnificent display of discipline, focus and determination. It was evident then that the youth were hungry for success; and were playing as a team with a mean streak, a characteristic long lost within the Test team.

It didn't require much prompting for the pundits to connect the victory of the youth to the glory days of the seniors in Tests and ODIs two decades ago. There were endless references to their joy on the field and dignity in victory. They played tough cricket, showed no fears, and went after all oppositions with confidence. As the tournament progressed they grew stronger in the mind and on the grass. By the final, they were looking like winners, and this imagery was communicated to the Indian 'top dogs' who seemed subdued and slightly fearful.

The teenage pace attack was hostile. Windies boys extracted bounce from the pitches, and used this circumstance to run into the faces of the Asian team. This too brought back memories of the Test team of the 1980s that instilled fear in the heart of Asia, Sunil Gasvaskar notwithstanding – the last great player left standing in the assault!

Islam did not agree with the explanation for success offered by CWI, both president and director of cricket operations. CWI spoke of the special preparations offered the youth before their arrival in Bangladesh. The frequency of training camps conducted was cited as a core basis for the special performance. The assumption presented was that camps built character, and that the teens responded to these exercises with alacrity. The team, however, did play poorly in the early round of the competition. Islam was more accurate in stating that the 'beauty of their win wasn't in their preparation, but in their execution at crunch moments.'[6]

Islam has called for a 'decoding' of the teens' talent. This implies that a secret script probably exists, and if found and deciphered, would reveal hidden truths. The assumption also is that their 'success story' is phenomenal, out of character, and beyond the imagination. They were not expected to occupy the top tier; there was certainly no bets placed on their reaching the top spot. Islam, therefore, was intuitive in calling for a decoding.

The 'execution of crunch moments', as processes of perfection, bears examination. Islam insists that 'there were pockets where an inevitable collapse looked a possibility' but instead the teens responded with 'serenity and confidence that belied their age.' This is a remarkable insight, not only in terms of its generosity and grace, but in its acknowledgement that Windies understood what was required and responded rationally. 'At no stage,' he said, 'did they look nervous'. Instead, what they showed was 'the hunger to succeed'. He continued: 'Equally impressive was their ability to think outside of the box. You could sense their changed mindset and approach,' he concluded.[7]

There has been no such description of Windies Test cricket in 20 years. Islam stands against the tide and offered something entirely unexpected and unfamiliar. He saw a rare species, and spent time describing the delight. His arrival at this crossroad must not go unnoticed. He too has to be decoded, and brought to the bar for cross examination.

Islam's description of Windies teens shows knowledge of all aspects of the game. Critically, it reveals that he is possessed of a mind that pays attention to departmental details. His commentary took the reader through the twists and turns of each game, as he recognized moments in their specific context. With these skills he sets about to assess the mind of young men as they read and reacted. He found them alert, and their thinking acute. He was excited by their youthfulness as a factor in agility of intellect.

Islam connects these variables into a narrative that presents a mind at peace even while at work. 'They started slowly,' he said, 'but found their bearings when it mattered.' Not since C.L.R. James has such perceptive, softly incisive, and graceful prose been constructed to expose consciousness as the key factor in performance. The poetic charm of his reasoning sets him apart on Valentine's Day when love was showered by a scribe upon a visitor who took the prize away from his principality. His nation was defeated yet his writing was victorious.

Then came the finale; the moment and admission that matters most. 'There is plenty of talent underneath the surface in the Caribbean,' he uttered. This was the end of the encryption that revealed that which was in doubt, or not known. There is 'enough talent' under Windies tent to take them beyond the gloomy horizon. What the success story yields, he threw out as he departed, is this: 'there is a tremendous amount of talent', and 'a group of teenagers have now shown the way'. The manner in which they constructed this victory 'said much about their awareness which should win a lot of praise.'[8]

Against the backdrop of Islam's call for a 'decoding' came Tony Cozier's intervention. He painted a reality image too deeply ingrained to be easily eradicated. The team had not yet won the final. Cozier's assessment came after their semi-final defeat of Bangladesh, a victory which he admitted was 'heart-warming in desolate West Indies landscape.' Yet Cozier saw little hope in the teens' rise to the top. The Windies 'A' Team, the next logical stage in their evolution, Cozier said, is 'nearly defunct', and 'the contracts issue is destroying the senior side'. In sum, then, there is no hope for these young stars, and chances are, he concluded, they will not be the basis of a Windies return to Test and ODI competitiveness.[9]

Unlike Islam, Cozier saw the Under-19 victory as representing but a 'whiff of optimism'. Where the former saw the potential for structural transformation and an eruptive evolution, the latter saw a layer of 'sweet smelling air' that will blow out as it blew in. Then came Cozier's dampening denouncement: 'It doesn't necessarily follow,' he said, 'that success at youth competition leads to success at the higher level.' Surely, given that Australia and India have won it three times must raise a discourse of causality in respect of their dominance in senior cricket.

There is also the matter of attrition, Cozier added, which is more a Windies than global problem. 'Once they outlive the age limit,' he said, 'some top teens drift away from the game into other pursuits; others won't develop sufficiently to qualify for Test or limited overs selection.' Cozier's media colleagues, however, saw enthusiasm in the teens' success. It was experienced in the commentary of Ian Bishop, Windies legend, and attributed to a 'widespread desire for a Windies revival.'[10] Commentators were happy to note that the youths' aggressive batting brought back memories of Windies Test 'heyday', and reported how pleased they were to 'see a West Indian team with such talent, play with such conviction.'[11]

Beyond Cozier's doubt, flatness of comprehension and cynicism remain the divisive world generated by the WIPA's world view that defines the Test team. Unable to examine the seminal aspects of youth success he stayed imprisoned by the WIPA's war on CWI:

> The obvious questions now are whether the players can carry the benefits of such experiences forward to first-class and eventual international level, and whether their best can somehow be kept away from the financially enticing clutches of mushrooming T20 franchise tournaments. Lack of opportunity, the slow, turning pitches in the Caribbean, and most of all the prolonged strained relationship between the WICB and players remain hindrances.[12]

He doubted that from the darkness of two decades of Test decline could come a shining light to show the path to a more fertile future. He was unable to see beyond the boundary that is littered with litigation, industrial relations confrontation, and ultimately the triumph of 'cash over country'.

There was undoubtedly an extraordinary sense of pride and satisfaction within Windies as a result of the winning of the ICC

(Author) presenting a book to teenager Kraigg Brathwaite for outstanding performance (2008)

Vice Chancellor's Cricket Match 2007, St Kitts – Floyd Reifer (L) and Chadwick Walton (R) coach and captain of the Combined Campuses and Colleges Team (after the game against England in 2017, St Kitts)

(Author sitting front left as Principal) with the victorious University of the West Indies Campus Team on winning the Barbados Premier League for an unprecedented four consecutives times. (2012)

With Chris Gayle who played in my official retirement match from the University's team, 2016, UWI, Cave Hill Campus, Barbados

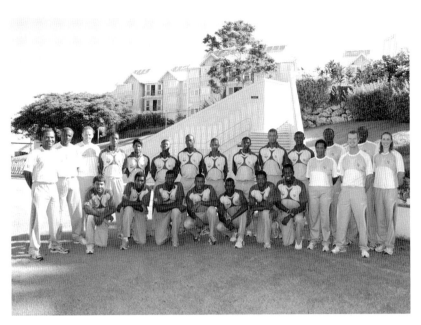

(2010) Inaugural Cohort of the WICB student cricketers at the High Performance Centre, The University of the West Indies, Barbados. Front row, 3rd form left, current Test Captain of the Windies, Jason Holder.

Author showing West Indies batsman/wicket keeper, his student, Chadwick Walton, how the defensive stroke is played, UWI, 3Ws Oval, Barbados (2015)

The two Hilarys: Author with Hilary "Larry" Gomes (centre) and Professor Clement Sankat (left) UWI Principal, St Augustine Campus, hosting the Zimbabwe Team in 2010.

University students in the West Indies Team at Kensington Oval (L to R) Carlos Braithwaite, Keswick Williams, Rovman Powell, Jonathan Carter, (centre coaches) Chadwick Walton, Jason Holder, 2016

Under-19 World Cup. Everywhere, there was conversation that spoke to a seismic shift. In the streets, boardrooms and political platforms, the result was seen as an expression of what is possible in a better managed, less toxic, cricket environment. There was the ultimate assertion that the victory is best seen as a metaphor for a generation of youth yet untainted by the real WIPA world. Cozier signalled the significance of this reasoning when he ended his commentary by stating that 'it is pertinent that the boys in Bangladesh don't yet have to concern themselves with contracts, T20 leagues and their relationships with CWI. Such potential problems,' he surmised, 'lie ahead'.

Windies youth environment, then, is defined by a paradigm that promotes the gold of performance innocence rather than the glitter of more money and less victories. The youth were celebrated for their demonstration of a thesis that illustrates this truth: that in the West Indies there is an abundance of natural talent which is mismanaged, spiritually decentred by the WIPA, and not allowed to fulfil its potential. CWI–WIPA war was a core problem that suppressed the resource, and diverted it along dangerous, unsustainable avenues. The buck has to end somewhere, and the most obvious place is CWI.

The 'abundant natural talent' thesis, however, is simultaneously attractive and flawed – though not fatally. It is true that Windies youth have been in the top tier of global cricket all along. But notions of their greater natural talent should have resulted in more winning performances – certainly ahead of India and Australia. The truth is, however, that they have generally been more competitive during the past two decades than the Test team. This raises two significant questions. Why the considerable disparity between youth and Test performance? How is it that superior natural talent at Under-19 transitions to inferior performance at Test level? The assumption is that senior teams of most countries are constituted of the former youth cohort. It also assumed that youth progresses along an officially designed growth path and that a given performance outcome can be explained in terms of compliance or deviance from this predictable trajectory.

It is generally agreed that the 'thing' which enables predictable progress along an approved path is the programme. Despite the effort of the UWI's cricket academy, Windies has an inferior programme in respect of addressing this challenge. Top Test playing nations have credible, professional programmes designed to transition youth players over the post-19 turbulence when attrition is at the highest peak. England's rise from the base to the top of Test rankings in the past 15 years, as well as Australia's ability to sustain their excellence, reside in the presence of a sophisticated, results oriented academy programme.

The instrument used to give effect to these outcomes is the cricket academy. In the Windies this initiative remains territorially divisive and riddled with anti-development rhetoric and reasoning. Many legends have dismissed the idea of an academy on the basis that they became performance superstars without the assistance of such. It is also frequently stated that academies promote paper performances while the game is played on grass. The general unawareness of many Windies legends about the performance promotion content of academies illuminates their insufficient formal education that results in a rejection of scientific approaches and data. Yet, they are very influential at official levels where policies are conceived and implemented.

CWI's dismantling of the HPC, and its subsequent closure in 2015, has had a negative impact on youth cricket. The Under-19 youth success had much more to do with the prior training of this cohort than with pre-tournament preparation. The players themselves understand this and have said so. They have regretted not being allowed to enjoy the academic and practical benefits of the HPC. CWI's error in diminishing and closing the academy functions under the guidance of Director of Coaching, Richard Pybus, must be corrected in order to sustain youth success.

There is undoubtedly more to the ending of the HPC than appears on the surface. The arrival of Pybus as cricket director coincided with the decline and decay of the high performance programme that produced both captain and vice-captain of the Test and T20 teams respectively – Jason Holder and Carlos Brathwaite. Both players also illustrated their talents within the set-up of the CCC.

Caribbean governments have called for the dismantlement and restructuring of CWI as a necessary prerequisite for the rise of Windies in Test. They have argued that on account of its general mismanagement and specific operational culture, a toxic environment surrounds player–officials relations. It has become endemic and serves to suppress performance outcomes. CWI has rejected this reasoning while suggesting that winning of the Under-19 World Cup as well as the T20 World Cup are proofs of its success.

CWI has also added that Test performance decline is attributed more to politicians' willingness to allow players to place 'cash before country' – unlike their counterparts in competitor countries. A 'stand-off' exists, and has become a tri-lateral debacle – players, state and officials splintered and polarized. The public discourse has served to expose young players to perspectives and information at a tender age, which will enhance their maturity and build a more decisive consciousness.

The Under-19 youth, contrary to Cozier's assumptions, are more politically informed and many have already made up their minds about the path they will take. The notion that they represent an 'innocence' about to be corrupted by the WIPA, and the pending lure of cash and anti-country actions is flawed as it failed to recognize that the youth are alert to the lessons of the era of endless litigations. Also, they have experienced the celebration of the legends of the golden era and the shame heaped upon the attitude and antics of recent 'stars' who bask in their own glow while darkness surrounds them.

The youth, then, are more focused and fiercely determined than at any moment since the monument fell. When Captain Holder celebrated these emerging players it was within the context of recognizing in them the elements he will need to get the job done at the Test level. He watched them closely because his search for matured consciousness and skill is no different from that of Captain Clive Lloyd and Viv Richards three decades ago.

The signs of scientific thinking are evident as is the commitment to leadership as the critical resource. This Fourth Windies Rising will be carefully crafted. The fear that endless pitfalls are waiting to claim the youth is real, not because officials have failed to pave a better path, but because this youth cohort is more politically aware and alert than its predecessor.

16

IMPERIAL CRICKET COUNCIL: REPARATIONS FOR WINDIES

The ICC adopted an unethical attitude towards Windies cricket that became a global eyesore within communities concerned with justice. Its reputation as a cabal of professionals without concern for the core values of the game was widely recognized. It has been hostile to Windies Test cricket in the era of its decline. This much is now common conversation; the call for corrective action is universal. Errant ears occupy its halls, and despite the growing Mexican wave of resentment against its anti-Windies attitudes, it remains placid behind panes of glass in its gluttony.

The Windies Test brand, one of the ICC's finest assets, is downgraded on its balance sheet. Captured by a corporate clique of Anglo–Australian moneymakers and Indian investors, it functions as a fellowship of cash in which those within the inner circle are fed, and those outside, despite their contribution, are marginalized and impoverished. This unethical circumstance resonates everywhere in the case of Windies that has done so much for the Test game.

Windies are paying a very high price for their principled positions over near a century. Its legacy was built on placing the public first; to entertain and to carry them on a journey to excellence. To show the world how the game should be played as a serious, cultural spectacle has been their contribution. Fans the world over have recognized the Windies way as a gold standard. Windies have served the game well, built it up and delivered a modern product. They have not only entertained but mentored the cricket world.

Everywhere the Test game is loved, respected and celebrated Windies contribution is recognized, and not in a glib, superficial fashion, but in terms of laying the foundations for what is today a rapidly growing sporting enterprise. No other nation, since England up to the 1940s, has done as much to take the game's art and science to the world. From the 1950s to 2000, global communities have carried Windies heroes in their hearts. They became synonymous with cricket excellence and the iconography of high performance.

There are reasons why the global transformation of the game centred the Windies. These nations made their greatest, single cultural investment in the game. For a century, Windies players set out to master the craft and to share their journey lovingly with fans, pundits, and critics alike. To love Test cricket was to admire Windies. The game took on a new, democratizing demeanor in their hands and they carried this case with dignity and determination.

These investments Windies made in world Test cricket should not be taken lightly. Neither should the ICC continue to be indifferent and hard-nosed in the face of the facts. Gratitude, it is often said, is the finest of virtues. The cricket world knows it owes Windies 'back pay', but the ICC constituted as an elite club, does not wish to acknowledge this special debt. It is an attitude born in the backward elements of Empire that remains dominant despite a century of liberation. It is a posture perfected by the English within its imperial order that says we have extracted because it's our right to do so; there is and will be no remorse or reparations. The debt is dismissed, and the injustice persists.

Windies went all out to save world Test cricket from a slow death after the Second World War. The Anglo–Australian hegemony of the prior half century had done wonders, but beyond that the game was grinding to a slow and boring demise. In England, the homeland of 'Test', the performance culture was deemed by the populace to be dull and uninspiring. Beating the visiting colonials was not enough. The natives wanted to see more art with the science, theatre as well totals. The smell of death and destruction after 1945 surrounded Test cricket. The dismissal from Downing Street of Winston Churchill, hero to the war, was proof enough that the English wanted to move on to a brighter, more inspiring day. Cricket they wanted to be a part of the journey.

C.L.R. James described English post-war Test cricket as addicted to the bare, basic survival, the minimum for the masses who had been fed the crumbs of imperial glory. But after fighting a war far too 'domestic' to be distant, the British realized that the world beyond their boundary carried within it the seeds of their salvation. They had seen the dazzling sight of Learie Constantine in club and county matches across the country; they were amazed, bamboozled, and driven wild by his style that was simultaneously Caribbean in cultural flair and form yet familiar in mood and method. Constantine was the Caribbean appetizer. The 'main' course was quickly served in the 1950s in the form of the 3Ws.

If the English admired Constantine as the game's first global showman, the stage performer of the inter-war Test game was George Headley. Therefore, they held a special place for Frank Worrell, Everton Weekes and Clyde Walcott. Worrell was the master of form and shape; he was the perfect cricketer. It was he who provided the leadership and vision the postwar Test game needed. He was the living embodiment of the game in need of a new mandate and mission.

It was no simple matter that Windies produced the world's most loved, revered and idealized cricketer. It was more than a major accomplishment for a nation relatively new to the turbulence of Test. Frank Worrell was the new culture carrier. He was the emerging consciousness of the game, its centre of gravity. He took possession of its heart, and offered humanity a sporting chance to put the terrible world war behind it, and to move on with an enlivened new, moral order. While Sir Winston Churchill was rejected at the polls as a relic of the old order, Sir Frank was celebrated as Britain's symbol of the new cricket spirit.

The Worrell discourse also took root in Australia, India, South Africa, New Zealand, and of course, in his Windies home. He represented excellence in every way; on the field he did it all. In each aspect of a Test he was not easily matched; his leadership off the field captivated the world's imagination and elevated the game to a higher level of respect.

The wisdom expressed in Worrell's oratory was what the world needed to hear; to give legitimacy to the post-imperial implosion that insisted upon the equal ethnic dignity of the human person. Grace and charm were his opening salvos, followed by inspiring insights and a soft but piercing intellect in his reading of the future. His personal touch was noble; his gifts of communication were uncommon and utterly empowering. Sir Frank was Windies golden gift to the game when it needed it most.

Then came his clone: Sir Gary Sobers! The combination of King and Prince enabled the world to stand still, in awe. The prince of the perfect play took to the global stage and made the script of cricket drama so titillating that the Test game soared in popularity. To witness the young Sobers was beyond sobering; it was transforming of consciousness and revolutionary in all segments of reason. He was simply unbelievable – unimaginable.

The greatest all-round cricketer the world has ever seen had arrived – a gift from the ghetto of old, colonial Bridgetown. As the prince of performance, he told the world that the game was his to reinvent. It was his rightful claim to appease the passions of landlord and labourers. In India, where his fleeting foot movements were recognized, and England that knew the ontology of his choreography, to Australia where grit and guts are admired, he offered grace and style. He took to the Worrell stage and unleashed upon it a love of the game that was to reign supreme.

The Worrell–Sobers axis was Windies' answer to the game's post-war environment. For 30 years, in the aftermath of a defeated imperialism, the game's emerging modern values revolved around Windies world vision. Then came Sir Viv Richards, the lion that stood up against the legacies of colonial injustice and gave the game a renewed political purpose it needed to stand up against racial bigotry that still haunted humanity. Viv's was a vision to level the global space. No privileges and special doors could entice him. He walked to the crease to give cricket a democratizing agenda that all post-colonial people recognized and desired. At home, he was the warrior knight standing against the elitism of imperialism.

Windies, then, in short order, gave cricket a King, a Prince, and a dozen Knights. Together they represented the soul of a future world that wanted to move on from the veneer of Victorianism that was no longer a stimulant to global aspirants. Windies offered a concrete answer when racialism had been exposed and dismissed. The rise of multi-racial cricket teams was their project. They brought truth, justice, and art to the centre of cricket; this has been the legacy of Windies investment in the world.

The ICC is now custodian of this Windies cricket legacy. The children of India play and laugh with joy in the parks, and do so in the culture of the game crafted under Windies watch. In Australia, they have grown to respect the tough but fair elements Windies insisted were critical development values. The English know more about Windies redesigning and saving their domestic cricket than they are willing to admit.

For these and related reasons the cricket world, still moral and magnificent in its mentality, stands against the ICC's insistent that Windies pay a punishing price for their financial poverty. There is a discursive disconnect between the moral world of cricket and the ICC's universe. It is a chasm that cricket will not survive unless brought to closure. It is not sustainable because everywhere the commonwealth of the ICC is pitted against the debt owed Windies. But there are reasons, not related to cricket, that are standing in the way. These must be discussed and dissolved before a new ICC dispensation can rise in which an investment in the Windies Test project can be conceptualized.

Scyld Berry, the British cricket writer whose pedigree is well respected, makes best the case against the ICC on behalf of Windies cricket and the future of a development enterprise. He does not sidestep the view that Windies woes are 'partly self-inflicted', but gives primacy to the point that they have more to do with a 'lack of ICC investment'. He begins his analysis with the governance model at the ICC and described how, a year ago, 'the Big Three of Australia, England, and India altered its constitution so that the bulk of the future revenue – well over half – would go to them, the three that need it least. Their maxim: each according to his greed.'[1]

But Berry does not end there. He accuses the ICC of creating a cabal culture in which Windies, and to some extent Pakistan and Zimbabwe, are marginalized and systemically discriminated against. The ICC, frankly speaking, says Berry, is anti-Windies and this is part of the 'injustice in this new order.' Injustice is not a word to be banded about lightly within the context of the global governance of an old sport. But Berry, like many other observers, can see clearly how the ICC's policies and attitudes are anti-Windies at a time when it needs from the governing body leadership and support.

Windies are the most financially challenged team of all the major Test cricket nations. Against the background of its extraordinary global contribution, the mean spiritedness of the ICC strikes Berry as creating an immoral order. The relative poverty of Windies is seen clearly in terms of the technological backwardness of its facilities. 'They need academies, and bowling machines,' he adds, 'and only financial investments can resolve this problem. They do not have the cash in hand, and the ICC seems unwilling to invest.'[2]

Berry insists upon a discussion of the central moral issue facing ICC's leadership of global governance. 'The ICC should be hands on enough,' he said, 'to make sure that some of the money goes into the pockets of West Indies cricketers.' They remain underpaid in comparison with their competitors from more developed economies, yet their contribution to the game is unmatched. The decline in Test performance of the team can be arrested, he concludes, but only a 'new-look, wise and generous ICC' can stop the rot.[3]

That the ICC is in a good financial position to invest in the primary legacy team is well understood across the cricket world. Ajit Vijaykumar, looking at the 'imbalance in world cricket financing affecting smaller nations', concludes that the 'ICC need to solve financial imbalances hampering West Indies and other nations'. His analysis speaks to the rule of greed and anti-Windies attitude at the ICC that threatens to destroy the very existence of the legacy member. The existence of a 'vast gap in the salaries of Test cricketers from Australia and the West Indies' is now common knowledge, he concludes, but less understood is the extent to which it prevents Windies from fielding their best Test team, and the negative impact on performance.[4]

Vijaykumar tells us that in early 2016 the Aussie cricketer was getting 'around $11,000 per Test while Caribbean cricketers get half as much. The difference is a lot more in the annual retainer of contracted players with a top Aussie getting $1 million and the best West Indian getting $140,000 at the most'. Windies Test Captain, Holder, calls upon ICC to establish 'some sort of resource pool which guarantees a minimum wage for Test cricketers'. The ICC must consider the vision that informs this proposal.[5]

This is unlikely to happen, however, as Vijaykumar agreed with Berry that the recent 'revamp of the ICC' saw India, Australia and England taking 'financial control' at the expense of Windies and other economically smaller nations. The ICC, he concludes, 'is not doing what it was expected to do'. Everything the ICC does forces Windies deeper into a pit of disrespect, as if the ICC wishes to see Windies grovel the way Tony Greig had expected in 1976. The ICC sees Windies, as it does other now designated 'small nations', as lining up for 'leftovers'.[6]

Steve Waugh, the highly effective captain of Aussie cricket during the period of Windies collapse, recognized the enormous contribution of Windies cricket, and is equally critical of ICC's attitudes. In his opinion the ICC seems prepared to allow Windies

Test 'to wither and die on the vine'. The ICC, he insists, has a responsibility to work through the economic factors involved, and ensure that Windies Test cricket 'get back to the level they were at'.[7]

Waugh's proposition to the ICC is consistent with that made by many other former players. Windies best players have abandoned Test cricket because of its inferior financial package. The ICC, he proposes, should standardize Test cricket fees across the board so that players from weaker economies are as well paid as those from stronger economies. The skill sets are not far apart, but salary scales are, hence the economic injustice against Windies it encourages.

David Gower, England's captain during the period of Windies highest performance, recognizes that the West Indies as a financially 'poor country' is paying the highest price in the current structure of world cricket under the ICC's arrangement that enfranchises 'elite' economic nations and disenfranchises all others. The ICC, he says, is a 'club in the clouds', and while he believes that it can and will do little to change the situation, the Windies as a Test nation are in a financially 'ridiculous' situation.He calls upon the governing body to find 'parity to help encourage everybody to play Test cricket for their respective countries', knowing full well that the West Indies is the only nation not in a position to enforce the principle.[8]

Michael Clarke, recently retired Aussie Test Captain, believes the ICC's finance structures have created a 'club versus country crisis' that is the greatest threat to Windies Test cricket. Unleashing the power of club cash, the ICC has refused to facilitate member nations such as Windies who struggle to keep Test cricket as a top priority. By opening spaces for club cricket to cash in on player talent, he argues that ICC's facilitation has enriched players from developed countries at the expense of Windies.

The refusal of ICC to 'find a balance' is read as a form of benign hostility to Windies, driven in part by executives who have either experienced career challenges against the Windies, or are carriers of racist attitudes towards black stars. While Clarke did not take his conversation in this direction, globally there is growing suspicion about the race attitudes of ICC executives. He recognizes, however, that 'a lack of money in the Caribbean game is seen as a key factor for many senior players turning their backs on Test to chase the riches on offer in T20s', but declares that 'international cricket has to be the priority'.[9]

Kevin Pietersen, former England Test star, believes that the ICC should step in and act in the best interest of the Test game. Windies players, he suggested, are still among the most talented in the world, and the ICC should ensure that they receive 'the same financial incentives to play Tests'. The West Indies, he said, 'doesn't govern cricket'. It is the ICC, he argues, that should develop a strategy to propel Windies stars back into the Test game.[10]

It didn't require more evidence to persuade Chinmay Jawalekar to conclude that in addition to some internal Windies industrial relations issues 'the ICC is to be blamed for this debacle.' The ICC, he said, makes decisions that are 'driven by the interests of the Big Three – India, England and Australia – and poor West Indies clearly does not feature in their plans'. Their proposals for future competitions are designed to further marginalize Windies, and everything they do, he says, carries a logic 'which can possibly mean that West Indies might slide further downhill.'[11]

Furthermore, Jawalekar, said, the 'ICC have also cut down the amount that they will distribute to West Indies cricket significantly, which means that the board is left with less money to pump into the system. The constantly repeated statement after every West Indies loss that 'world cricket needs a strong West Indies,' he said, has become a cliché. He continued:

> But for a strong Windies, WICB needs to put a decent infrastructure in place – state of the art academies, coaching facilities, physiotherapists, counselors, mental conditioning coaches, et al. – which is essential to address their problem of not producing quality cricketers... Unfortunately, all this is very expensive. That is where ICC and wealthier boards need to step in.[12]

Clive Lloyd understands this circumstance all too well. He was the lead architect of the Windies third rising. As chief selector in 2013, he experienced much of the backlash from ICC executives, some of whom suffered at his hands in their playing days. Also, those administrators, who paid a price in terms of facing their national anger on returning from a Windies trashing, are now observing Windies struggling at the bottom.

Lloyd knows better than anyone the psychology terrain within the ICC, and the attitudes of its executives who are mostly former cricketers of modest records. He admits that 'a lack of finances', and the lure of the T20 cricket cash, 'are the main factors tearing apart West Indian cricket', but feels powerless to respond in the face of ICC's intransigence. He fears that the 'T20 competition has probably decimated' Windies Test cricket, but recognizes that a 'cash injection from the ICC' would allow it to 'stay viable as an international [Test] force'.[13]

Reflecting on the ICC's financing strategies, Lloyd affirms the opinion that 'the current financial structure sees the rich nations get richer and the poor ones poorer.' He concedes that it is hard for the Windies to survive under such a model.' While not suggesting that Windies have a right to special financing outside of what is best for world cricket, he does suggest that in Windies' glory days world cricket benefited more democratically. Yet, the ICC has adopted a new strategy that is assured to see the Windies fall rather than rise.[14]

The intervention of the Federation of International Cricketers Associations (FICA) in the 2014 Windies players pull out from the India tour, served to re-centre the inadequacy of ICC's attitudes to cricket development in the Caribbean. The stern rebuke by the ICC of Windies players was within reason, but the inadequacy of the response illustrated its limited perspective on the root cause of the case at hand. Chairman N. Srinvasan's statement concerns more than it reveals:

> It was undoubtedly a sad chapter in our sport. It damaged cricket's integrity and reputation, as well as affecting confidence within the

cricket community, especially that of the fans. The ICC Board was determined to address this situation and ensure that such incidents never happen again. The ICC is working with the concerned members towards finding a positive resolution and is confident that there will be constructive outcomes for our games.[15]

But what is significant, according to FICA, is that the ICC moved to address only 'part of the problem', and indicated that 'more must be done'. Tony Irish, executive Chairman of FICA, informed the media that while he accepts that 'international cricket has reasonable protection against arbitrary and unexpected player actions, if the ICC really wants to deal with the whole problem then it should look to do more than simply taking action against players.'[16]

The restructured ICC moved away from the Future Tours Program (FTP), and consolidated the big revenue tours among the 'big three', leaving the Windies in the lower levels of what is called the revenue racket of the elite. The FTP provided a predictable and sustainable revenue stream for Windies. The role of the ICC was to ensure that a minimum schedule of two Tests and three ODIs were at the core of each tour over an eight-year cycle of home and away. High performance teams could not, therefore, sideline less achieving teams, providing a democracy of access to recovery while facilitating equitable revenue distribution.

Since the ICC coup was effectively consolidated in April 2014, and world cricket since then managed by a corporate cabal, national boards are free to settle tours on a bilateral basis. This has raised serious concerns, says, FICA, 'from less financially stable nations', such as Windies, 'that they will be isolated in the new system'. Already, this fear is being realized, and Windies are aware that the new ICC structures and policies have weakened their ability to survive with dignity. FICA shares the Windies perspective that 'international cricket should not be based simply on bilateral agreements' and has called upon the 'ICC to have a hand in ensuring members meet their touring responsibilities.'[17]

These developments have generated an impulse within Windies to distrust the ICC's intentions, and to be generally suspicious about its motives in consolidating power in the hand of the richer nations. The creation of an anti-Windies environment that supports unequal and inequitable revenues, against the background of Windies' enormous legacy contribution to world cricket, is undoubtedly driven by a desire not to halt further Windies Test decline. There are no surprises here. In the 1990s, the ICC was on an anti-Windies warpath at the policy level when 'bring down the Windies' sentiment infiltrated its corridors and burst into its boardrooms. Every pundit in the pavilions of the world can read this script, and the global view that resonates within public consciousness is that the ICC continues to see the Windies as a non-favourite.

Windies, then, face a strong headwind on the Test field and on the ICCs committees. Starved of an equitable share of the pie it had enlarged, it enters the game with less technical preparation and empowerment. Bereft of basic technologies for postmodern training and development, the Test teams seem systemically sidelined on the field of play. The ICC's revenue regime contributes to the rigging of this inequality. Its hands off, indifferent stance on Windies Test decline, raised eyebrows in the past; now it raises rage!

A counter-revolution by members who are committed to a return to an equitable environment is required. Windies should lead this agenda as it has paid the greatest price. CWI should form coalitions with other disenfranchised nations, and other ethical, even if elite nation, in challenging the disrespectful dollars first, policy within the ICC. It should, furthermore, do this in the spirit of the democracy it had done so much to foster when it was called to influence proceedings. The world we have lost at the ICC was a world crafted in large measure by Windies. CWI's duty is to restore its legacy of equity.

There is growing support at the ICC for a strategy to return to an environment dedicated to equity, and to move away from the domination of elitism. The long-term health of the Test game requires that it consolidates its ethical foundations in strategic planning for the future. The dollars diplomacy of the bilateral negotiations of tours has torn into the financial viability of Test teams from poorer economies that are unable to meet parity with their deepening inequality. The ICC must not be allowed to lose sight of its remit to treat all members fairly and equally. At this time, it is in breach of this ethical culture. There has to be accountability, and CWI should lead the campaign for compliance with these traditional core principles.

The election of Shashank Manohar as chairman of the ICC in June 2016 was expected auger well for the counter-revolution. His campaign for the post was based on support for the ethical principles of equal rights within the ICC's membership. There was broad-based celebration of his election, especially as he publicly indicated his opposition to the 'big three' clique that has done so much damage to Windies cricket and the global game in general.

Manohar declared an intention to honour his campaign objectives and promises. In his election success, there was hope for Windies Test culture. If he failed, Windies was expected to fall further into the ICC's festering feudalism that he had challenged. Windies do not call for handouts and charity. The call is for a level field on which to play, the kind of environment in which they have flourished. The ending of ICC's hostility to Windies success and Test legacy is part of a necessary ethnic and ethical cleansing of the organization.

Much depended on Manohar's resilience and resolve. To repair the damage done is the meaning of the term reparations. The ICC owes Windies a debt of gratitude. It owes them reparations. Manohar's sudden, shocking resignation, has thrown the discourse of justice at the ICC into disarray. Windies is in need of a new advocate to champion its reparatory justice cause.

Summary

The rise and fall of Windies Test cricket as a competitive force is one of modernity's most specular cultural experiences. As a perfectly executed project, the rise attracted global attention far beyond the boundary of the sport, and resonated with communities that varied enormously in their appreciation of the game as an athletic practice.

After 50 years of Test engagement, Windies were recognized in 1967 as world Test champions, a status they quickly lost but regained in 1978 and held for near 20 years. The unprecedented eruption and dominance set them apart as transformational leaders and elite cultural performers. They were motivated by forces emanating far beyond their sport, but within the boundary a spellbinding professionalism became their hallmark.

Driven to perfect and dominate the sport by a soul rooted deep within their history of oppression and injustice, Windies Test cricketers came to represent and symbolize what the twentieth-century world was demanding – greater freedom, respect, justice, equality and cultural integrity. They symbolized ideological practices that were much more than sporting performances. They were iconic leaders of an alternative intellectualism that gave primacy to principles sweeping away the rubble of dying colonialism. Empowered by these winds of change, Windies Test cricketers soared beyond the standard performance parameters of the game and created a space they alone could occupy. It was a collective effort fashioned into a formidable force by brilliant performers.

By the mid-1990s, the edifice had cracked and within a decade had crumbled. The collapse equally captured the global imagination while tearing at the consciousness of an economically declining post-colonial society. The Caribbean world, unable to embrace the sense of despair, called for an explanation that would be consistent with both external and internal circumstances. This monograph is a response to the call.

Accounting for the loss of excellence in any society is no simple matter, particularly within the context of a highly competitive activity such as sport. Many perspectives have been offered and these, I hope, have been fairly assessed and commented upon. The thesis offered here, within the context of a diversity of opinion, is that the detachment of Windies cricket culture from the process of nation building within the broader framework of sports globalization and industrialization, established the basis for the significant reduction of Test performance quality.

The alignment of eligibility, availability and player performance within the new market economy of international cricket, forced Windies Test cricketers to consistently choose between 'country' and 'cash' priorities. Windies emerged as the only Test team that could not assure its fans that the best players would take the field. The option of playing commercial cricket transcended Test cricket, and with this came Dinanath Ramnarine's blistering scorched-earth industrial relations leadership of WIPA that threatened the existence of the enterprise

De-politicized, decentred and dollarized, Windies Test cricket was destabilized and subsequently diminished. Without its supportive socio-political and cultural scaffold, the structure of excellence was weakened. Lacking ideological energy beyond themselves, the Test team took upon itself an identity of fragmentation and demotivation – an assembly of cricketers without a cause.

Drawn mostly from working-class communities that have been financially ravished by the austerity of the International Monetary Fund's programmes and World Bank structural adjustments, young cricketers found it difficult to identify with a region which they were socialized to see as hostile. Unable to rise with alacrity, it was a simple matter to place all social and ideological aspects of national representation at the lowest levels of priority. With the eruption of 'each cricketer for himself' as the ruling principle, Windies Test appeared a selected outfit without a soul. The 'green' of cash displaced the 'maroon' of the Test as the overarching, overriding deciding colour. Without a soul to support the journey from the bottom, the Windies Test team not only seemed vanquished but content in their languished state.

Restoring the vision has become the priority of pundits and development agencies, such as The University of the West Indies that created an academy culture in order to create critical consciousness and innovative choices. Within this programme was developed a new mental construct that seeks to celebrate the legacy of Test excellence. Critically, it has generated a significant anxiety among young Test players to restore that which had been lost.

Within this context, it is possible to imagine the return of Windies to the peak of Test performance. The evidence of the return journey is discernible. Preparation has been made. The soul is being restored.

Postscript

The Patterson Report sets out the past and future of CWI in elegant and insightful terms. CWI has been a solid, senior partner in the 'Enterprise of the West Indies'. In the creation and consolidation of a culture of West Indianness its legacy is greater than that of most other regional institutions.

From its inception in 1927, CWI has been a critical part of the agenda to forge the nation-building project from the rubble of rejected colonialism. With roots sunk deep in the imperial ethos, and its branches bearing the burden of nationalist aspirations, CWI, has produced the sweetest West Indian fruit of the twentieth century. Sadly, as it is currently structured, it is not fit for 21st century purpose.

CWI governance design and functions are in need of conceptual and concrete reform. But its resistance efforts serve only to win a greater number of adversaries. Critics are prepared to set aside its considerable prior contribution and their increasing anger is generating a crescendo of public rage. Inability to accept its inadequate public accountability says that society is secondary. No organization that discharges an enormous public duty and function should be left to report only to itself, even if constituted as a private corporation.

Corporate leaders have long found pathways into the presidency of CWI. The business reputations of Sir Errol Dos Santos in the 1950s and Jeffrey Stollmeyer between 1974 and 1981 constituted precedents for Patrick Rousseau. But it is Rousseau's regime, 1996 to 2001, that is directly associated with the rise of the cash driven corporate culture that coincided with the fall of Windies as a competitive Test team.

The mandate given Rousseau was clear enough: bring 'big cash' into Windies coffers, end the amateurish administration era at CWI and inaugurate contemporary corporate commercialism into the cricket culture. He was invited to transform the then WICBC from a traditional non-governmental organization (NGO) into corporate managerialism. His election was interpreted as an invitation by investor interests to privatize the pulse of the Windies heartbeat. Rousseau's rule, then, was welcomed by cricket commercialists as a turning point in the transition to the 'cash before country' paradigm that inadvertently created the context for Test players' withdrawal of committment triggered the performance implosion of the Windies Test team.

The powerfully symbolic capitalist maximization agenda culture associated with the Rousseau regime radically revised the relations between the WICBC and players, and between players and the public. While it is true that it takes two hands to clap for more cash, it requires but one type of mind to imagine and manage the millions.

Board and players were united in celebration of the incipient cash culture, but from the outset were deeply divided over the ownership and distribution. The contradictory financial forces unleashed by the 'more money mandate' immediately produced a management calamity that brought Windies Test cricket into disarray.

Board and players sung from different sheets, producing an ominous overture that signifies more fury than unity. The influx of crates of cash led to a crash of care for the culture of Test cricket. Each side has insisted upon the rightness of its claim for a greater share. Meanwhile, the spectator lost confidence in both to retain a balanced sense of purpose. Each side sought to assert its public political power over the other as Test series were lost one after another.

The past two decades of decline and despair have seen the evolution of a popular consensus that the WICB should undergo governance reform or face political rejection. The thesis that it is the only regional institution that presides over a public good but has no effective external stakeholder representation is strongly supported by the evidence. The proof is within both its procedures and its administrative arrangements. In 2017 it was rebranded as CWI.

CWI reports to itself. Over time, it has brought on board a few 'non-territorial directors' who serve at the pleasure of the President. These additional voices, though very valuable, do not represent a significant departure from the essential truth that the organization is distant from the societies it serves. It stands combatively between the game it administers and the societies that produce participants. It is now described by the public as a pariah.

The persuasive perspective of the Patterson Report lies in its call for an external Council of Stakeholders to which the President and Board report on their leadership and governance. Such a body would be constituted as an expert panel chosen to assure the effective mobilization of appropriate mentalities and skilful management in order to promote growth and development as well as access and accountability.

As a document that could determine the modernization of CWI's management, the Patterson Report represents a lifeline to the future. It seeks to resolve the core problem within Windies Test cricket; CWI is the only employer who cannot place its best team on the field on account of a breakdown in relations between itself and its employees.

Any reform imperative of CWI must be discussed in terms of the growth of its considerable private power and its diminished sense of public purpose. While the trajectory of its increasing private power in the age of cricket globalization has administratively alienated its players, its floundering sense of social purpose has equally excluded and ignored the public interest. Its manner of late has been to display its authority without regard to societal sensitivity which accounts for the public inclination to assume its guilt in every conflict with players. Even when the public feels the wrongness of player perspective, it is prepared to support them over the Board.

CWI has undoubtedly lost considerable credibility and legitimacy in the public mind despite its grand historic legacy of achievement. This has more to do with the use of its private political power than with its presiding over failed efforts to regain Test competitiveness.

As the creation of a new player consciousness takes form, the reform of CWI is necessary, urgent and right. Its refusal to facilitate this process has resulted in citizens' call upon governments to impose a new dispensation. Heads of governments led principally by Prime Ministers Ralph Gonsalves and Keith Mitchell have been explicit: good governance of Windies is in the public interest and the role of the state is to ensure this objective.

Captain Jason Holder has called for balance between the competing forces of market globalization and Test duty. Such a progressive state of stakeholder sensibility will require a corresponding consciousness within the corporate corridors of CWI. It will take the reform of both sides in order to reconstitute Windies as one enterprise. The captain has captured the context; it is for the president to promote the content. Effective, passionate leadership on the field requires the sustainable support of the Board. Mutual trust must be created.

The old player order has been wiped away by WIPA, yet it remains fully intact at CWI. This breach of synergy is the root cause of endemic conflict. A reformed CWI is a critical part of the effort to effectively restore the sold Windies soul. It is not a matter of choice but of responsibility. As it approaches in 2027 a century of public service, CWI must be restructured to constitute its corporate power as a source of public purpose. If this test is failed, the people of the region can say goodbye and adieu to their greatest collective investment in nation-building.

***

There is more to the bat than meets the ball. The pain of the West Indians who no longer pour into grounds to see their Test team penetrates beyond the boundary of their bodies. The cry is for greater accountability and better public governance. The cure resides within the field of community and national consciousness and the raising of levels of institutional commitment.

West Indian society is an ancient element of the political centre of that which is known as the West. Ripped of its resources by centuries of colonization it continues to reside in its economic South. The persistence of post-colonial poverty accounts, in the end, for the pain that is carried by each patron into Test pavilions.

'Cash before Country', the organizing principle that erupted, took centrestage, and guided the demise of Windies Test excellence is not therefore a cricket metaphor. It is the pillar of a post nationalist ordering of everything that reflects the abandonment of the earliest frameworks of nationhood.

The concern here is as much with monitoring the buckling of West Indian societies under the weight of three decades of IMF tests as it is with explaining two decades of West Indian Test cricket performance paralysis. Test cricket for nearly a century has occupied a special place at the high table of Caribbean intellectual conception of its independent self. It has been part and parcel of the family furniture. The recent selling of the silver by both senior and junior members of the family was in effect the first phase of an incipient global philosophy that proclaimed the disposal neither a heresy nor a horror.

Restoring the proud and pristine legacy of Test is simultaneously an expression and a requirement of the next phase of West Indian nationhood. It requires first and foremost a return to respect for the virtue of pride in ancestral performance. Young citizens are required to rise upon the basis of innovative, indigenous forms of reasoning and to see beyond the immediate despair of endemic failure. They alone can confront the causes of decay and decline, and effectively rupture and reject the philosophy of their predecessors.

This was the cricket project the University of the West Indies undertook as a top priority for the public good. For over two decades it has stayed attached with tenacity. It resides at the centre of the new consciousness that is driving the agenda for the next rising in Test cricket. While considerable turbulence still persists around the university's role within sections of CWI's management, the seeds for success have been sown. There is no turning back. The vision and its implementation are already bearing fruit.

Effective post-national leadership is a scarce commodity in communities struggling to overcome global vulnerability and historical dispossession. For this reason public institutions in developing countries like those in the Caribbean, perhaps more so than elsewhere, cannot afford the wastage and wreckage associated with routine rejection and abandonment of best practices established by previous administrations.

With 'regime change' the prior leadership is waved on with envy and suspicion. How easily it is when structures are weak to sacrifice signs of success on the altar of ego; and how simple it is to speak of an alternate vision without minimum merit or maximum meaning.

Rebuilding the culture of Test cricket fell to the leadership of the High Performance Centre within the learning environment of the host campus. The Julian Hunte administration of WICB understood the need to resist ravishing subversive schemes that desired Tests best laid to rest, and buried in a coffin of T20 cash. But Test retained the full blessings of the core of Caribbean collective conscience.

Training a cohort of conscious cricketers, smart enough to see the importance of balance, was top priority. The success of this project would require an effective academy function in which plenty cash and poor communities could coexist and facilitate the restoration of public pride in field performance.

Young Test cricketers would be trained to reconnect to the principles that drove the vintage success of Windies, and relate to the mentalities that meticulously managed the relationship between player, community and country. While honing and developing technical skill and competence, the academy programme rested upon values such as professional responsibility and collective leadership.

The West Indies Test team on its way to England in 2017 is a carve-out of the HPC's first cohorts forged within the academy environment. They represent a conceptual break in the thinking that matured in the Lara–Gayle era. Their mentoring is carefully crafted and their exposure to high performance technical and professional training is not at the expense of a sense of public purpose.

The core of the first two cohorts of academy trained Test players is fast reaching maturity. Ten of those selected to tour are programme graduates: Captain Jason Holder, Kraigg Braithwaite, Jermaine Blackwood, Miguel Cummins, Shane Dowrich, Shannon Gabriel, Kyle Hope, Shai Hope, Kieran Powell and Raymond Reifer. This core will be the seed of the next rising of Windies Test cricket. This was the strategic plan. This is the vision that has guided their emergence and presence.

The first unfortunate feature of the Cameron presidency of the CWI was the winding down and ultimate closure of the Sagicor–WICB High Performance Centre. The explosive ending of the academy was as tragic as it was trivial. Even in the context of a 'fix it don't finish it' discourse the decision laid bare the basis of the sustainable rise of the next generation that has shown signs of extraordinary energy and intellectual engagement. The High Performance Academy must be forthwith restored and repositioned to facilitate the next generation.

After Holder's generation, then what? West Indian fans walking through the gates know the perils of poor leadership and its expression in personal vilification instead of public illumination. Behind Holder there is an abundance of ability looking to cricket Academies for the ammunition their parents saw displayed. The CWI is required to invest in such frameworks and facilities.

More than the results of Test matches is at stake on this tour to England. Holder's men, young heroes in the struggle to reverse the view that West Indians should reside at the bottom, will stop the rot and rebuild the base. But the next rising of the Windies Test enterprise will be the task of those who follow.

Notes

Introduction

1. C.L.R. James, *Beyond a Boundary* (London: Hutchinson, 1963); Michael Manley, *A History of West Indies Cricket* (London: Andre Deutsch, 1988); see also, Paul Buhle, *C.L.R. James: The Artist as Revolutionary* (London: Verso, 1988).
2. Hilary McD. Beckles and Brian Stoddart, eds., *Liberation Cricket: West Indies Cricket Culture* (Manchester: Manchester University Press, 1995); Hilary McD. Beckles, ed., *An Area of Conquest: Popular Democracy West Indian Nationalism* (Kingston: Ian Randle Publishers, 1994); *A Spirit of Dominance: Cricket and Nationalism in the West Indies* (Kingston: University of the West Indies Press, 1996); see also 'Beyond C.L.R. James's "Beyond a Boundary": From Liberation and Nationalism to Globalization and Commodification in the West Indies,' in *Beyond CLR James: Shifting Boundaries of Race and Ethnicity in Sport*, ed. John Nauright et. al., 7–17 (Fayetteville, AR: The University of Arkansas Press, 2014).
3. Hilary McD. Beckles, *The Development of West Indies Cricket, Age of Nationalism, Vol 1* (Kingston: UWI Press, 1998); '[Brian Lara: (Con)testing the Caribbean Imagination,' in *Sport Stars: The Cultural Politics of Sporting Celebrity*, ed. David Andrew and Steven Jackson, 243–57 (London: Routledge, 2001).

Chapter 1: Ten Theories of Decline

1. 'West Indian Cricket: Gone with the Windies,' *The Economist*, December 19, 2015.
2. Ibid.
3. Ibid.
4. Ibid.
5. Ibid.
6. Eudine Barriteau, Sir Denis Byron, Deryck Murray, Dr Warren Smith and Dwain Gill, 'Report of the Independent Review Panel

on Cricket Governance,' CARICOM Cricket Subcommittee Report, 2015.

7.   The *Economist*, op.cit.

Chapter 2: Sir Gary: Tears of a Clone

1.   'Sri Lanka v. West Indies: Sir Garfield Sobers Brought to Tears by Windies' Plight,' *Fox Sports*, October 22, 2015.

2.   'Sir Garfield Sobers Breaks Down over State of West Indies Cricket,' *Mail on Line*, October 22, 2015, http://www.dailymail.co.uk/sport/cricket/article-3284867/Sir-Garfield-Sobers-breaks-state-West-Indies-cricket-going-struggling-long-time.html.

3.   Ibid.

4.   The *Economist*, December 19, 2015.

5.   Geoff Lawson, 'Sad Decline of West Indies Cricket Can't Be Arrested Without External Help,' *Advertiser*, December 5, 2015.

6.   Ibid.

7.   Ibid.

8.   The *Wisden Cricket Monthly*, December 1998 edition.

9.   Ibid.

10. Osman Samiuddin, 'Brian Lara Isn't Walking through That Door: Australia Set to Magnify West Indies Shambolic New Normal,' The *National Sport*, December 8, 2015.

11. 'Wills World Cup, Kenya v. West Indies at Pune,' *ESPNcricinfo*, February 29, 1966, http://www.espncricinfo.com/wi/engine/match/65175.html.

12. Martin Williamson, 'Kenya down the Lackluster Legends,' *ESPNcricinfo*, March 12, 2011, http://www.espncricinfo.com/magazine/content/story/505731.html.

13. Ibid.

14. Ibid.

15. 'Windies Maestro Calls for Wholesale Shake up,' *ESPNcricinfo*, September 5, 2000, http://www.espncricinfo.com/ci/content/story/94029.html.

16. Tony Cozier, 'The South Africans in the West Indies, 2000–2001,' *ESPNcricinfo*, 2002, http://www.espncricinfo.com/ci/content/series/61838.html.

Chapter 3: Passing IMF Tests: Losing Test Matches

1. See Beckles, *The Development of West Indies Cricket: The Age of Globalization*, vol. 2 (Kingston: UWI Press, 1998), 31–79.
2. Beckles, *The Development of West Indies Cricket*, op. cit;145–73.
3. Michael Manley, *A History of West Indies Cricket* (London: Andre Deutsch, 1988); also 'Cricket and West Indian Society,' in *An Area of Conquest: Popular Democracy West Indian Nationalism*, ed. Hilary McD. Beckles (Kingston: Ian Randle Publishers, 1994), 142–51.

Chapter 4: No More Heroes: Stars Only

1. Beckles, *The Development of West Indies Cricket* vol. 2, 115–43.

Chapter 5: The Empire Strikes Back: England's Revenge

1. Cited in Michele Savidge, *Real Quick: A Celebration of the West Indies, Pace Quartets* (London: Blandford Press, 1995), 179.
2. Ibid., 181.
3. Ibid., 157.
4. See Beckles, *The Development of West Indies Cricket* vol. 2, 94–100; *The Voice*, UK, 4 July 4, 1995.
5. Ibid., see also *Wisden Cricket Monthly*, July 1995, 10; Alistair McLellan, *The Enemy Within: The Impact of Overseas Players on English Cricket* (London, Blandford Press, 1944), 202–204.
6. Ibid.
7. Savidge, op.cit., 181, 185.
8. Ibid.
9. S. Rajest, 'Pace Like Fire: West Indies Battery of Fast Bowlers,' *ESPNcricinfo*, August 15, 2011, http://www.espncricinfo.com/magazine/content/story/527402.html.
10. Ibid.
11. Ibid.
12. Dileep Premachandram, 'Cricket's Turning Points: The Bouncer Rule,' *ESPNcricinfo*, December, 18, 2010, http://www.espncricinfo.com/magazine/content/story/491190.html.
13. Ibid.
14. The *Independent*, 'Bird Wants End to Bouncer Rule,' February 28, 1994, http://www.independent.co.uk/sport/cricket-bird-wants-end-to-bouncer-rule-1397077.html.

15. Sharda Ugra, 'More Bouncers Please,' *ESPNcricinfo*, December 9, 2012, http://www.espncricinfo.com/magazine/content/story/ 562185.html.

16. McLellan, op.cit.

17. Ibid.

18. Ibid., 108–109.

19. Colin Croft, 'West Indians Playing in English County Cricket Are so Few,' *Professional Cricketers' Association Online*, http://www. thepca.co.uk/west-indians-playing-in-english-county-cricket-are- so-few.html.

20. Ibid.

21. Ibid.

Chapter 6: Rise of Company Cricket: Test Divest

1. *Independent* (Trinidad), October, 25 1997.

2. Andi Thornhill, *Daily Nation*, September 9, 1997.

3. *Independent* (Trinidad), October 25, 1997.

4. Woody Richard, *Barbados Advocate*, September 17, 1997.

5. Andi Thornhill, *Daily Nation*, September 17, 1997.

6. *Daily Nation*, October 8, 1997.

7. *Express* (Trinidad), October 28, 1997.

8. Ibid.

9. Ibid.

10. *Express* (Trinidad), October 29, 1997.

11. *Sunday Sun* (Barbados), November 23, 1997

Chapter 7: From 'Whispering Death' to Dollar Diplomacy

1. See Martin Williamson, 'Who's Groveling Now? When Tony Greig Overstepped the Line on the Eve of England's Series against West Indies,' *ESPNcricinfo*, May 19, 2007, http://www.espncricinfo. com/magazine/content/story/134960.html; 'West Indian Cricket Team in England in 1976,' *Wikipedia.org*, https://en.wikipedia.org/ wiki/West_Indian_cricket_team_in_England_in_1976; Arunabha Sengupta, 'Cricket Rifts 14: When West Indies Made Greig's Life Miserable for Using Word "Grovel,"' *Cricket Country*, April 4, 2012.

2.   Greg Buckle, 'Cricket World Cup 2015: Michael Holding Pleads with Windies Batsmen to Start Using Brains,' The *Daily Telegraph*, March 7, 2015.

3.   See Chris Barratt, 'Australia v. West Indies: Curtly Ambrose Reads Riot Act to Team before Test,' The *Camberra Times*, December 9, 2015.

4.   Nagraj Gollapudi, 'Players Must Show Some Loyalty to Our Cricket,' *ESPNcricinfo*, January, 13, 2015, http://www.espncricinfo.com/westindies/content/story/820501.html.

5.   Ibid.

6.   Ibid.

7.   Tony Cozier, 'Are West Indies T20 Stars Keen on Returning?' *ESPNcricinfo*, June 14, 2015, http://www.espncricinfo.com/magazine/content/story/887449.html.

8.   'T20 Competitions Destroying West Indies Cricket: A Crying Sobers,' *Sportzcentre*, October 22, 2015.

9.   Ibid.

10. 'Gibson Criticizes Senior Players,' The *Gleaner*, March 24, 2011.

11. Ibid.

12. 'Chris Gayle Hits Back at Coach Ottis Gibson for Criticizing West Indies,' *Daily News and Analysis*, March 24, 2011, http://www.dnaindia.com/sport/report-chris-gayle-hits-back-at-coach-ottis-gibson-for-criticising-west-indies-1523720; 'Holding Lambast WICB, Gibson over Handling of Senior Players,' *Jamaica Observer*, May 25, 2012.

13. 'Brian Lara Urges Windies to Give up on Current Generation,' *IBC News*, December 11, 2015.

Chapter 8: Rousseau's Rebels: The Tour That Sold the Soul

1.   Martin Williamson, 'When Lara Led a Players' Strike,' *ESPNcricinfo*, February, 23, 2013, http://www.espncricinfo.com/magazine/content/story/605998.html.

2.   Ibid.

3.   Rick Eyre, 'Misunderstanding Sorted and West Indies Tour is on,' *ESPNcricinfo*, November, 10, 1998, http://www.espncricinfo.com/ci/content/story/76822.html.

4. 'The West Indies in South Africa, 1998–1999,' *ESPNcricinfo*, http://www.espncricinfo.com/wisdenalmanack/content/story/153410.html.
5. Ibid.
6. Ibid.

Chapter 9: Lara: Prince Who Should Have Been King

1. *Daily Nation*, Barbados, April 10, 1996.
2. See Wes Hall, 'Manager's Report of the 1995 West Indies Tour of England,' Reproduced in *Trinidad Guardian*, December 8 and 12, 1995.
3. See Beckles, *The Development of West Indies Cricket*, vol. 2, 19.
4. Ibid.
5. Tim Hector, 'On Lara and the Captaincy,' *Trinidad Express*, December 10, 1997; also, ibid., 131.

Chapter 10: Gayle: Star Who Should Have Been a Hero

1. Anna Kessel, 'Chris Gayle Willing to Quit West Indies Captaincy and Face Future without Test,' The *Guardian*, May 12, 2009.
2. Ibid.
3. 'Chris Gayle is WIPA Cricketer of the Year,' *PTI*, Trinidad, June 6, 2011.
4. Elijah Anatole, 'WICB, CEO; Chris Gayle Despite Not yet Settled,' *St Lucia Star*, April 2, 2012; 'No End to Gayle Charade,' *Daily Express*, October 29, 2011.
5. Ibid.
6. Steve James, 'Chris Gayle Must Be Sacked as West Indies Captain,' May 16, 2009, http://www.telegraph.co.uk/sport/cricket/international/westindies/5334960/Chris-Gayle-must-be-sacked-as-West-Indies-captain.html.
7. 'Chris Gayle Reappointed for Australia Tour,' *ESPNcricinfo*, November 2, 2009, http://www.espncricinfo.com/ausvwi09/content/story/432696.html.
8. 'WICB Statement on Meeting with Chris Gayle,' June 14, 2011, http://www.windiescricket.com/node/2490.

9. 'WICB Drops Disciplinary Charge against Gayle,' *ESPNcricinfo*, July 16, 2015, http://www.espncricinfo.com/westindies/content/story/899419.html; 'WICB Lets Chris Gayle off for Rant against Selectors,' *Znews*, July17, 2015.

10. 'We Can Get the Best out of Gayle: Renegades,' December 17, 2015, http://www.cricket.com.au/news/chris-gayle-melbourne-renegades-david-saker-bbl05-big-bash-league/2015-12-17.

Chapter 11: Ramdin Rams Richards: Bravo Berates Windies

1. 'Viv Blast Woeful Windies: Says Ramdin Has Deteriorated,' *SK Cricket*, May 29, 2012.

2. 'West Indies Come after T&T and W.I.,' *Hindustan Times*, March 27, 2010; 'Bravo Puts Windies behind T&T and Mumbai,' Sports Max.tv.

3. Ibid.

4. 'W. Indies Chiefs Slam Bravo as India Cricket Tour Called off,' *Yahoo News*, October 17, 2014.

5. Ibid.

6. 'Dwayne Bravo Says West Indies Pull out Had Everybody's Consent,' October 25, 2014, http://www.cricketcountry.com/news/dwayne-bravo-says-west-indies-pull-out-had-everybodys-consent-202432

7. Nagraj Gollapudi, 'Samuels Wanted to Finish India Tour, Bravo "Shocked,"' *ESPNcricinfo*, October 25, 2014, http://www.espncricinfo.com/westindies/content/story/792267.html.

8. *Yahoo News*, October 17, 2014.

9. Ibid.

10. '1st ODI is Scheduled to Commence,' *Press Trust of India*, October 8, 2014.

11. Tony Cozier, 'West Indies Still Reeling from India Pullout,' *ESPNcricinfo*, Sepember 27, 2015, http://www.espncricinfo.com/magazine/content/story/923667.html.

12. Ibid.

Chapter 12: Back to the Future: Educate, Negotiate, Don't Violate

1. See Beckles, *The Development of West Indies Cricket* vol. 2, xv–xvi.

2. Ibid., 161–67.

Chapter 13: Holder's Hope: Finding the Balance

1. Cited in *Daily Nation*, January 12, 2016.
2. Ibid.
3. Ibid.
4. See Tony Cozier, 'Where Next for West Indies as a Test Team?' *ESPNcricinfo*, December 13, 2015, http://www.espncricinfo.com/magazine/content/story/951937.html.
5. Ibid.
6. Ibid.
7. Mark Nicholas, 'Is it Time for the West Indian Nations to go it Alone?' *ESPNcricinfo*, December 17, 2015, http://www.espncricinfo.com/magazine/content/story/952847.html.
8. Ibid.
9. Ibid.
10. Ibid.
11. Ibid.
12. 'Lara Backs Holder to Lead Windies in All Formats,' *ANI News*, December 21, 2015.
13. Chris Barratt, 'Country Must Come First,' *Sidney Morning Herald*, January 2, 2016.
14. Ibid.
15. Ibid.

Chapter 14: The Empire Exposed: The Nerve of Nicholas!

1. Mark Nicholas, 'Is it Time for the West Indian Nations to go it Alone?' ESPNcricinfo, December 17, 2015, http://www.espncricinfo.com/magazine/content/story/952847.html.
2. Ibid.
3. Most Hon. P.J. Patterson, Sir Alister McIntyre and Dr Ian McDonald, Final Report, Committee on Governance of West Indies Cricket, October 2007.

Chapter 15: Preparing for the Fourth Rising

1. 'West Indies under-19 Cricketers Win World Cup,' The *NY Carib-News*, Februrary 16, 2016.

2. George Dobell, 'Contract Crisis Threatens West Indies on Eve of World Twenty20,' *ESPNcricinfo*, February 9, 2016, http://www.espncricinfo.com/icc-world-twenty20-2016/content/story/971003.html.

3. Ibid.

4. Ibid.

5. Mohammad Islam, 'Carty, Paul steer West Indies to Under-19 glory,' *ESPNcrickinfo*, February 14, 2016, http://www.espncricinfo.com/icc-under-19-world-cup-2016/content/story/972461.html.

6. Islam, 'Decoding the West Indies Under-19 Success Story,' *ESPNcricinfo*, February 14, 2014, http://www.espncricinfo.com/icc-under-19-world-cup-2016/content/story/972771.html.

7. Ibid.

8. Ibid.

9. Tony Cozier, 'Under 19 Success Heartwarming in Desolate West Indian Landscape,' *ESPNcricinfo*, February 14, 2016, http://www.espncricinfo.com/magazine/content/story/972521.html.

10. Ibid.

11. Ibid.

12. Ibid.

Chapter 16: Imperial Cricket Council: Reparations

1. Scyld Berry, 'Demise of West Indies Cricket…," *Telegraph* UK, February 16, 2015.

2. Ibid.

3. Ibid.

4. Ajit Vijaykumar, *Sports 360*, January 4, 2016.

5. Ibid.

6. Ibid.

7. Daniel Lane, 'Steve Waugh Urges ICC to Save Windies and Preserve Test Cricket,' *Sidney Morning Herald*, January 19, 2016.

8. 'David Gower Advocates 4-day Test,' *Cricket Country*, January 31, 2016, http://www.cricketcountry.com/news/david-gower-advocates-4-day-tests-to-reignite-passion-in-format-390210.

9. 'ICC Should Fix West Indies Club vs. Country Row, says Michael Clarke,' *NDTV Sports*, December 19, 2015.

10. Andrew Ramsey 'Lloyd, KP Laments Player Exodus to T20,' *Cricket Network*, January 1, 2016, http://www.cricket.com.au/ news/clive-lloyd-kevin-pietersen-west-indies-australia-chris-gayle-andre-russell/2016-01-01.

11. Chinmay Jawalekar, 'ICC and World Cricket Must Intervene and Save the West Indies Cricket,' *Cricket Country*, December 14, 2015, http://www.cricketcountry.com/articles/icc-and-world-cricket-must-intervene-and-save-the-west-indies-cricket-367052.

12. Ibid.

13. Ben Horne, 'Clive Lloyd Says Cricket Australia Hamstrung West Indies Preparation,' The *Daily Telegraph*, January, 1, 2016.

14. Azad Ali, 'Lloyd: Windies Need International Help,' *Caribbean Life News*, January 12, 2016, http://www.caribbeanlifenews.com/ stories/2016/1/2016-01-15-azad-lloyd-cricket-cl.html.

15. 'ICC War against West Indies Repeat,' *ESPNcricinfo*, November 9, 2014.

16. Firdose Moonda, 'FICA Chief Calls for Return of FTP,' *ICC News/ ESPNcricinfo*, November 10, 2014, http://www.espncricinfo.com/ ci-icc/content/story/798021.html.

17. Ibid.

Select Bibliography

Anderson, Benedict. *Imagined Communities*. London: Verso 1991.

Axford, Barrie, and Richard Huggins. 'The Telemediatization of Cricket: Commerce, Connectivity, and Culture in the Post-television Age.' In *Cricket and Globalization*, edited by Chris Rumford and Stephen Wagg. Newcastle: Cambridge Scholars Publishing, 2010.

Bairner, Alan. *Sport, Nationalism and Globalization*. New York: State University of NY Press, 2001.

Baksh, Vaneisa. 'The Stanford Plan.' ESPNCricinfo, October 27, 2005.

Bateman, A., and J. Hill, eds. *The Cambridge Companion to Cricket*. Cambridge: Cambridge University Press, 2011.

Beckles, Hilary McD. *The Development of West Indies Cricket: The Age of Nationalism, vol 1*. Kingston: University of the West Indies Press, 1998.

———. *The Development of West Indies Cricket: The Age of Globalization, vol. 2*. Kingston: University of the West Indies Press, 1998.

———, ed. *An Area of Conquest: Popular Democracy and West Indies Cricket Supremacy*. Kingston: Ian Randle Publishers, 1994.

———, ed., *A Spirit of Dominance: Cricket and Nationalism in the West Indies*. Kingston: UWI Press, 1998.

———. *Mastering the Craft: Ten Years of Weekes, 1948–1958*. Kingston: Ian Randle Publishers, 2007.

———. 'The Detachment of West Indies Cricket from the Nationalist Scaffold.' In *The Cambridge Companion to Cricket*. Cambridge: Cambridge University Press, 2011.

——— and B. Stoddart, eds. *Liberation Cricket: West Indies Cricket Culture*. Manchester: Manchester University Press, 1995.

Birbalsingh, F. *The Rise of West Indies Cricket: From Colony to Nation*. London: Hansib, 1996.

Constantine, L. *Cricket and I*. London: Philip Allan, 1933.

Dirlik, A. 'Rethinking Colonialism: Globalization of Postcolonialism and the Nation.' *Interventions* 4, no. 3 (2002): 428–48.

Eagar, Patrick, and Alan Ross. *West Indian Summer: The Test Series of 1988.* London: Hodder and Stoughton, 1988.

Featherston, M., ed. *Global Culture: Nationalism, Globalization and Modernity.* London: Sage, 1990.

Fraser, David. *Cricket and the Law: The Man in White is Always Right.* London: Routledge, 2005.

Gemmell, J., and B. Majumdar, eds. *Cricket, Race, and the 2007 World Cup.* London: Routledge, 2008.

Giulianotti, R., and R. Robertson. 'Sport and Globalization: transnational dimensions.' In *Globalization and Sport*, edited by R. Giulianotti and R. Robertson. Oxford: Blackwell, 2007.

Gupta, A. 'The Globalization of Cricket: The Rise of the Non-West.' *International Journal of the History of Sport* 21, (2004): 257–76.

Haigh, Gideon. 'The Indianisation of Cricket.' Cricinfo.com, July 23, 2008.

Holding, Michael. *No Holding Back: The Autobiography.* London: Weidenfeld and Nicolson, 2010.

———, and Tony Cozier. *Whispering Death: The Life and Times of Michael Holding.* Kingston: West Indies Publishing, 1993.

Holton, R. *Globalization and the Nation-State.* Basingstoke: Macmillan Publishers, 1998.

James, C.L.R. *Beyond a Boundary.* London: Hutchinson, 1963.

———. *The Future in the Present: Selected Writings.* London: Allison and Busby, 1977.

Kaufman, J., and O. Patterson. 'Cross-National Diffusion: The Global Spread of Cricket.' *American Sociological Review* 70 (2005): 82–110.

Khondker, Habibul. 'Globalization, Cricket, and National Belonging.' In *Cricket and Globalization*, edited by Chris Rumford and Stephen Wagg. Newcastle: Cambridge Scholars Publishing, 2010.

Lee, Mark. 'The $55 Dollar Question: Whither West Indies Cricket?' *Abeng News Magazine*, January 9, 2009.

Lister, Simon. *Supercat: The Authorised Biography of Clive Lloyd.* Bath: Fairfield Books, 2007.

Bibliography

Malcolm, D. 'It's Not Cricket: Colonial Legacies and Contemporary Inequalities.' *Journal of Historical Sociology* 14, no.3: 253–75.

Malcolm, D., J. Gemmell and N. Mehta. 'Cricket and Modernity: International and Interdisciplinary Perspectives of the Study of the Imperial Game.' *Sporting and Society* 12, nos. 4–5 (2009): 431–46.

Manley, Michael. *A History of West Indies Cricket*. London: Andre Deutsch, 1988.

Marqusee, Mike. *Anyone but England: Cricket and the National Malaise*. London: Verso, 1994.

McLellan, A., ed. *Nothing Sacred: The New Cricket Culture*. London: Two Heads Publishing, 1996.

———. *The Enemy Within: The Impact of Overseas Players on English Cricket*. London: Blandford, 1994.

Nauright, John et al., eds. *Beyond C.L.R. James*. Fayetteville, AR: The University of Arkansas Press, 2014.

Oliver, Brian. 'Sport Gears up for Global Revolution,' The *Observer*, October 28, 2007.

———, and R. Gillis. 'Games without Frontiers.' The *Observer*, October 28, 2008.

Pandaram, Jamie. 'We Need a Champion: The Scheme to Rescue Tests.' *Sidney Morning Herald*, September 21, 2009.

Patterson, P.J. *Report of the Governance Committee on West Indies Cricket*. Kingston: West Indies Cricket Board, 2007.

Richards, V. *Hitting across the Line: An Autobiography*. London: Headlines Books, 1991.

Rumford, Chris. 'More Than a Game: Globalization and the Post-Westernization of World Cricket.' *Global Networks* 20, no. 2 (2007): 202–15.

Rumford, Chris, and Stephen Wagg, eds. *Cricket and Globalization*. Newcastle: Cambridge Scholars Publishing, 2010.

Sassen, S. *Losing Control? Sovereignty in an Age of Globalization*. New York: Columbia University Press, 1996.

Savidge, Michéle, and A. McLellan. *Real Quick: A Celebration of the West Indies Pace Quartet*. London: Blandford, 1995.

Steen, Rob. 'Acronym Wars: The Economics and Indianisation of Contemporary Cricket.' In *Cricket and Globalization*, edited by Chris Rumford and Stephen Wagg. Newcastle: Cambridge Scholars Publishing, 2010.

Wagg, Stephen, ed. *Cricket and National Identity in the Post-Colonial Age*. London: Routledge, 2006.

Weiss, Linda. *Globalization and State Power. Development and Society*. 29, no. 1 (2000): 1–15.

Wilde, Simon. 'IPL in a Fix: Lalit Modi is Going but a Whiff of Corruption Still Hangs over His League.' The *Sunday Times*, April 25, 2010.

———. *Letting Rip: The Fast-bowling Threat from Lillee to Waqar*. London: Witherby, 1994.

Index

The letter *t* following a page number denotes a table.